W9-AVS-306

The Selected Poetry of Vicente Huidobro

TRANSLATED BY

David M. Guss
Stephen Fredman
Carlos Hagen
W. S. Merwin
Geoffrey O'Brien
David Ossman
Michael Palmer
Jerome Rothenberg
Eliot Weinberger
Geoffrey Young

The Selected Poetry
of Vicente Huidobro

EDITED WITH AN INTRODUCTION

BY DAVID M. GUSS

A NEW DIRECTIONS BOOK

Copyright © 1963 by Empresa Editora Zig-Zag, S. A.
Copyright © 1976, 1977, 1979, 1980, 1981 by David M. Guss
Copyright © 1981 by Stephen Fredman
Copyright © 1981 by Carlos Hagen and David Ossman
Copyright © 1975, 1981 by Geoffrey O'Brien
Copyright © 1976, 1981 by Michael Palmer
Copyright © 1980, 1981 by Jerome Rothenberg
Copyright © 1975, 1980, 1981 by Eliot Weinberger
Copyright © 1976, 1977, 1981 by Geoffrey Young

All rights reserved. Except for brief passages quoted in a newspaper,
magazine, radio, or television review, no part of this book may be repro-
duced in any form or by any means, electronic or mechanical, including
photocopying and recording, or by any information storage and retrieval
system, without permission in writing from the Publisher.

This English-language edition is published by arrangement
with Señor Vicente García-Huidobro Portales, representing the heirs
of Vicente Huidobro. Illustrations in this edition by Pablo Picasso,
Juan Gris, and Hans Arp are reproduced with grateful acknowledgment
to the Huidobro collection.

Manufactured in the United States of America
First published clothbound and as New Directions Paperback 520 in 1981
Published simultaneously in Canada by George J. McLeod, Ltd., Toronto

Library of Congress Cataloging in Publication Data
Huidobro, Vicente, 1893–1948.
    The selected poetry of Vincente Huidobro.
    (A New Directions Book)
    Poetry in English translation, parallel
Spanish or French texts.
    I. Guss, David M.   II. Title.
PQ8097.H8A24   1981   861   81–4305
ISBN 0–8112–0804–4   AACR2
ISBN 0–8112–0805–2 (pbk.)

New Directions Books are published for James Laughlin
by New Directions Publishing Corporation,
80 Eighth Avenue, New York 10011

ACKNOWLEDGMENTS

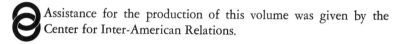Assistance for the production of this volume was given by the Center for Inter-American Relations.

Grateful acknowledgment is made to the following magazines and journals in which some of these translations originally appeared: *Chicago Review, Invisible City, Montemora, Panjandrum, Poems from the Floating World,* and *Zero.*

Acknowledgment is also given to the following for first publication of specific translations. The translation of *"La Poesía Es un Atentado Celeste"* ("Poetry Is a Heavenly Crime") by W. S. Merwin is taken from Merwin's *Selected Translations, 1968–1978* (Copyright © 1972, 1979 by W. S. Merwin), reprinted by permission of Atheneum Publishers. Jerome Rothenberg's translations of *"Tenemos un Cataclismo Adentro"* ("There Is a Cataclysm Inside Us") and *"Altazor de Canto I"* (from "Canto I of Altazor") first appeared in the anthology *Doors and Mirrors,* edited by Hortense Carpentier and Janet Brof, Viking Press, 1972. *"Solo"* ("Alone") as translated by David M. Guss and "Canto III of Altazor" as translated by Eliot Weinberger were originally published in *The Borzoi Anthology of Latin American Literature,* edited by Emir Rodriquez Monegal, Alfred A. Knopf, Inc., 1977. The Carlos Hagen-David Ossman translations were originally presented on KPFK, April 23, 1966, on the broadcast "Chilean Poets: Carlos Pezoa Veliz, Vincente Huidobro," produced by Carlos Hagen. Translations by Michael Palmer and Geoffrey Young appeared in the Sand Dollar Press edition of *Relativity of Spring: Thirteen Poems by Vicente Huidobro.*

The publisher and editor would like to give special thanks to Rosario Santos and David Unger without whose unfailing support publication of this volume would not have been possible.

The photographs in this edition were made available through the kindness of Dr. David Bary of the University of California, Santa Barbara, to whom grateful acknowledgment is given.

The Spanish and French texts of the poems included in this volume are used by permission of Señor Vicente García-Huidobro Portales and follow the standard versions of the *Obras Completas de Vicente Huidobro,* published by Empresa Editora Zig-Zag, Santiago, Chile, 1964.

MANY HANDS HELPED MAKE THIS BOOK:

To all the translators who contributed their work and support, to Uzelle Williams who read through it so often, to Fernando Alegría who so generously guided me along the way, to Hugo Montes who sent help from Chile, to Tom Raworth whose translation of the *Tres Inmensas Novelas* must await another volume, and to Howard Norman, Barbara Einzig, and Carolyn Harper who helped stoke the fires of my own enthusiasm—thank you.   D.M.G.

Contents

Introduction:
Poetry is a Heavenly Crime

I

"The first man flies to light the sky
Space bursts open in a wound"

While many North American readers are by now familiar with the
dark earth of Vallejo and the passionate seas of Neruda, the aerial
world of their most important contemporary remains little known in
this country. And yet in Latin America it was Vicente Huidobro who
opened the doors and retuned the lyre. It was Huidobro who "made
rivers run where none had been before." Latin American poets know
this. Octavio Paz calls Huidobro the "magnificent bird" and writes:
"He is everywhere and nowhere. He is the invisible oxygen of our
poetry." Huidobro knew this too. He wrote about himself: "At seven-
teen, I told myself, 'I must become the first poet of America.' Soon,
after just a few years, I thought: 'I must become the first poet of my
language.' Then, as time went on, my ambitions rose and I told my-
self: 'I must become the first poet of my age.'" As to the fulfillment of
this prophecy, Huidobro had no doubts. In a 1938 interview he said:
"Modern poetry begins with me." And then finally: "I am poetry!"

The "I" is a mythic one, a part of the heroic persona which
Huidobro assumed for himself. As in Whitman, it is a "self" transcend-
ing the ego, a public *mythos* evolving into commentary on the printed
word. The *mythos* created by Huidobro is a complex one. It is both
trickster and shaman, both clown and clairvoyant. It is "the one who
sees himself working and laughs at the other face to face."

Many have claimed that it is the fantastic legend of Huidobro that
has obscured the appreciation of his poetry, and it is true that scandals

and public controversy attracted as much attention to him as did the publication of his many books of poems, novels, plays, and essays. And so, perhaps it is only today—more than thirty years after the poet's death—that we can start to read his work without the distraction of the literary and political feuds with which it was initially received. And yet, the Huidobro legend is as important a part of Huidobro's work as was Rimbaud's flight to Africa or Duchamp's silence, for Huidobro saw himself as the total poet on the "ultimate frontier" of consciousness—the "demigod" on the epic quest for the infinite.

II

Vicente Huidobro was born in Santiago on January 10, 1893 into one of Chile's wealthiest families—a family of bankers and landowners who traced their lineage back to Burgos nobility:

> I am, through my ancestors, Castilian and Galician, Andalusian
> and Breton. I am Celt and Spaniard, Spaniard and Celt. I am an
> aboriginal Celto-Iberian, impervious and hardheaded, balanced per-
> haps by a touch of Jew.

He went to a Jesuit high school but dropped out very early after being reprimanded for reading Zola. With his mother's support, he began educating himself and writing his first verse. His mother was an important Chilean feminist and author who wrote under the pseudonymn of Mona Lisa, and it was with her help that Huidobro published his first book at 18, *Ecos del Alma* (*Echoes of the Soul*) and began the first of his many literary reviews, *Musa Joven* (*Young Muse*). His youthful poetry, which was later to embarrass him, was romantic, Catholic, and deeply rooted in the Modernist tradition of Ruben Darío which dominated turn of the century Latin American literature. And yet, by his second book, *Canciónes en la Noche* (*Songs in the Night*), he was already on his way to pioneering new forms with the development of the calligram.

Four more books in as many years (one of them, *Pasando y Pasando* [*Giving and Taking*] confiscated by his grandfather because of scandalous remarks about his family) and then:

The senseless mockeries, the unbreathable atmosphere, forced me to leave my native mountains and search for climates more favorable to gold prospectors.

However, Huidobro's vision of a new poetry, a poetry that doesn't "imitate the details of things but the constructive laws that form their essence and give it its own independence from everything else," was already solidifying.

His first stop was Buenos Aires. "It was there that they baptized me a Creationist for having said in my lecture that the first condition of the poet is to create, the second to create and the third to create." He also published what was to be his first book of Creationist poems, *El Espejo de Agua* (*The Mirror of Water*), in which Darío and the old school were laid to rest and the call for a new poetry was sounded.

From Argentina he sailed to France, the land of Baudelaire, Rimbaud, and Mallarmé. It was the middle of the First World War. Almost immediately, Huidobro found himself allied with the Cubists:

> It was the heroic epoch, in which we struggled for a new art and a new world. The thunder of the cannons didn't drown the voices of our spirit. Intelligence stood its ground, at least in France. I formed part of the Cubist group, the only one that's had a real importance in the history of contemporary art. In 1916 and 1917, I published in Paris, along with Apollinaire and Reverdy, the magazine *Nord-Sud,* which today is considered one of the principal organs of the great struggle for revolutionary art in those days. My closest friends were Juan Gris and Jacques Lipchitz. Lipchitz and I were the youngest in the group. They called me the *"blanc-bec,"* which could be translated as the Benjamin of the family. . . . Apollinaire would come to dinner on Saturdays. Max Jacob, Reverdy, and Paul Dermée would often come as well. Occasionally, Blaise Cendrars, Marcoussis, and Maurice Raynal would show up, just home from the front. Then I met Picasso who was returning from Southern France and about to put on the famous "Parade" ballet to the music of Erik Satie, another old and dear friend.

The call for a new art, based on its own intrinsic properties and not subservient to the imitation or reproduction of nature, was heard everywhere. In New York, where the Armory Show had already caused an uproar, William Carlos Williams, Mina Loy, and others were embarking on their own search for an art founded in "nature's active part." In Germany, Expressionism was being born. In Holland, Neoplasticism. In Zurich, Tristan Tzara and the Dadaists were starting to meet at the Café Voltaire. And in music, Schönberg, Satie, and Stravinsky were on their way to overturning the limitations of "functional tonality" and programmatic composition. Varèse called it "absolute music." Futurism was already considered passé.

Huidobro began to write in French. Coupled with his early reading of the Symbolists, his education and class background had led him toward a belief in the supremacy of French culture. It was a belief not uncommon to an aspiring South American writer at that time. The Chilean writer Fernando Alegría comments that "for a man such as Huidobro, who received an education among the upper class in Chile, his eyes were fixed on France. It was Paris. Becoming a great artist in France was the great triumph, *la consagración*."

In 1918 Huidobro went to Spain as an evangelist of the new poetry. Greeted as a hero, he set up a salon in his Madrid apartment. His visit led to the birth of a new movement in Spanish literature. It was called Ultraism and included among its followers a young Argentine writer named Jorge Luis Borges, who was at that moment stopping in Spain on his return home from Switzerland. Huidobro published four books during this stay—*Tour Eiffel, Hallali, Ecuatorial,* and *Poemas Articos*—as well as a second edition of *El Espejo de Agua.* By the time of his return to Paris, Apollinaire was already dead and he had broken with Reverdy over the authorship of certain poetic theories. The ensuing struggle with Reverdy made him consolidate his aesthetic ideas more than ever under the heading of Creationism. What had begun as a simple theory of poetry was quickly becoming a one-man school:

> For having affirmed and repeated, as a constant leitmotif, what my sole interest in poetry was—when I started to approach this level of creation of a new world—they called me a Creationist. A name I didn't invent and which at first I rejected because there was already a school of philosophy by that name and it had nothing to do with the aesthetic principles I espoused, which could lead to an absurd confusion.

Later, several people tried to dispute the title with me, and then I was forced to defend it.

Over the next six years Huidobro travelled throughout Europe, giving readings and lecturing on the aesthetic principles of Creationism. In 1921 he started a magazine called *Création* in which he was to publish some of his most important manifestos. The following year he held an exhibition of "painted-poems" at the Théâtre Edouard VII. The exhibit was called *Salle 14,* and although Huidobro had planned to publish these calligrams as a book, only two of them, "Moulin" and "Paysage," were ever printed.

It was during this period as well that Huidobro began his long involvement with radical politics. Through contact with the Irish resistance in Dublin, he was inspired to write a novel/tract against English imperialism: *Finis Britanniae: A Redoubtable Secret Society Directed Against English Imperialism.* It appeared at the end of 1923. Four months later Huidobro disappeared. When he returned after several days' absence, he claimed British agents had kidnapped him in an attempt to force a retraction. Many doubted his story and Huidobro fell into temporary disgrace. And so, after publishing his collected manifestos along with two books of French verse, *Automne Régulier* and *Tout A Coup,* he packed his bags and returned to Chile.

From Santiago, he began to promote his new poetic ideas throughout South America. Together with Jorge Luis Borges and the Peruvian Alberto Hidalgo, he published a large anthology of the new Latin American poetry. It was called *Indice de la Nueva Poesía Americana.* Huidobro's dedication is characteristic. It read:

To the true poets, strong and pure. To all the young spirits, free of base passions, who haven't forgotten that it was my hand that spread the seeds.

Huidobro also remained politically active, becoming the editor of the leftist newspaper *Acción.* After publishing a particularly bitter editorial against the ruling junta in August of 1925, he was beaten up by rightists and dropped on his doorstep with a fractured skull. The ensuing furor in the national press was enough to get him declared a candidate for the presidency by the Association of Students. Newspapers referred to him as the "Creationist Candidate."

Soon after, he began receiving other death threats, these from the family of a young woman named Ximena Amunategui whose father was the rector of the University of Chile. This affair was to change both his life and his poetry. For the moment, it was enough to break up his first marriage of almost fifteen years and force him to flee the country.

Returning first to France, Huidobro went on to New York where he was awarded a $10,000 film prize by the League for Better Pictures for his unpublished film-novel, *Cagliostro*. Lindbergh had just returned from Paris in triumph. *The New York Times* reported that Huidobro, the pioneer of "poetic aviation": "said he would give 50,000 francs of the money for the erection of a monument to American aviators."

Huidobro once again returned to Paris where he resettled with Ximena whose escape from her family in Santiago they had mysteriously engineered. The next several years were to be among the most prolific of Huidobro's life. He completed the final drafts on his great epic, *Altazor*, as well as work on his long prose poem, *Temblor De Cielo* (*Skyquake*). He also began work on a series of novels and plays: *Mío Cid Campeador, La Próxima* (*The Next One*), *Papá o El Diario de Alicia Mir* (*Papa or The Diary of Alicia Mir*), *Tres Inmensas Novelas* (*Three Immense Novels,* written in collaboration with Hans Arp), *En La Luna* (*On The Moon*), and *Gilles de Raíz* were all published within six years of each other.

With the premonition of another war (*La Próxima*) and the desire to be close to his ailing mother, Huidobro returned to Chile in 1933. By now Huidobro had stopped writing in French altogether. He had been accepted by the European avant-garde and was ready to assert himself on his own continent. His return was a triumphant one. Young artists and poets flocked to him, arranging art fairs and lectures. Huidobro began a series of short-lived reviews—*Total, Vital, Ombligo*—and participated in the formation of many others. But the center stage was not his alone. Pablo Neruda and Pablo de Rokha also had their followings and the three poets engaged in a vicious and perpetual feud with one another. And yet, it was Neruda and Huidobro who really dominated the world of Chilean poetry during the thirties. Theirs were the voices that sang loudest in a country wracked by depression and unstable governments, and despite their bitter rivalry, they found themselves allied in their sympathies for the Communist

Party. For during this period, both poets actively worked for the election of leftist candidates. Their political styles were as different as their poetic ones. Here's how Fernando Alegría recalls Huidobro during one campaign:

He would make a very impressive performance. I remember Huidobro very distinctly during a congressional campaign in Chile. I don't remember the year. This was probably in the early thirties—maybe '33 or '34. And I was interested in seeing Huidobro as a political person. I was a very young person at the time, a student, probably in the last year of high school or something like that. So I went to the theater. And the candidate was the owner of the theater, a man by the name of Pairoa. And he was a Communist candidate to become a representative—a member of the House of Deputies. And Huidobro was the main speaker. And people were expecting a really strong statement, a sort of high display of oratorical rhetoric. And Huidobro started talking in poetic terms. His speech was poetry. I remember very well. He was talking about *palomas* (doves): *"Las palomas, éstas salen de aquí de allá."* ("The doves come out from here and there.") It was a poetic statement. Very beautiful. And that, I'm sure, meant nothing to the people who were there.

The man was elected. But probably not on account of Huidobro's speech. People were talking about action, political action, and he was talking about poetic actions. Eventually maybe the two can get together, but not at the time he was speaking in Chile.*

In 1937, Neruda and Huidobro, along with scores of other poets of their generation, attended the International Writers' Conference in Valencia, Spain, in support of the Republican effort against Franco. It is said that their abuse of each other at that time was so extreme that an open letter was issued asking them to maintain peace in the interest of the Republic. Huidobro remained in Spain, purportedly in the uniform of a *miliciano,* but to what extent he participated in the fighting, no one seems to know. It is probable that he worked as a correspondent as he was to do only a few years later during World War II. However, here too, the Huidobro legends abound. One has him as the

* From an interview with Fernando Alegría, conducted by the author, January 31, 1976.

first combatant to enter Berlin, at which time he is reported to have captured the private telephone of Adolf Hitler.

After World War II, Huidobro retired from public view, becoming inaccessible to all but his closest friends. Disillusioned by three wars and exhausted by years of literary and political struggle, he withdrew with his third wife, Raquel Señoret, to his family estate of Llolleo, south of Cartagena on the Chilean coast. Many say these last years were bitter ones for Huidobro, that he was a *"poeta maldito,"* the "Citizen of Oblivion" going into seclusion "to be alone with the word." Whether this is true or not, it was a period of final reflection and illumination:

Now I know what I am and what I was
I know the distance that runs from a man to the truth
I know the word the dead love best
This is the one who wept the world the one who wept bright stars

At Llolleo, Huidobro wrote some of his most beautiful and moving poems, often as if already on the other side of death, "the one who went beyond death." The voice is different in these "last poems" and so is the style. There is a sense of urgency to reveal, a sense of last testament. Everywhere, death and time are confronted. Everywhere, silence is embraced.

In the heat of the Chilean summer, on the second day of 1948, Huidobro collapsed in the main square of Cartagena while carrying his bags from the train station. Partially paralyzed, he was carried by strangers to his home at Llolleo. By afternoon, friends began arriving from Santiago. From his bed, Huidobro called for a mirror, took one last look, and died.

III

I'm the mad cosmic
Stones plants mountains
Greet me Bees rats
Lions and eagles
Stars twilights dawns

Rivers and jungles all ask me
What's new How you doing?
And while stars and waves have something to say
It's through my mouth they'll say it
(*Altazor,* Canto I)

This is the poet summoning his spirits in the same way a shaman would. For Huidobro, poetry is just this invocation: a magic rite whereby "man puts himself in contact with the Universe, discovers its sense of unity, turns himself into a small God, and makes his cosmos." The poet is once again "maker," and "Creationism" is meant in the most literal sense of the word: the creation of "new worlds that never existed before, that only the poet can discover." The discovery is of the "inner word—the magic one." Huidobro claimed that the inspiration for his poetic theories came from the words of an Aymara Indian poet who said: "The poet is a God. Don't sing about rain, poet. Make it rain!" The poet was to be a sorcerer of language, endowed with the supernatural powers to create "separate realities":

> We've accepted, without greater thought, the fact that there can be no other realities beyond those surrounding us, and we haven't believed that we, too, can create realities in a world of our own, in a world awaiting its own flora and fauna. Flora and fauna which only the poet can create, through that special gift which Mother Nature has given him and him alone.

The poet was to be the new culture hero—a Prometheus who would not only create "new worlds" but also new and "liberated" humans through the reenactment of the primordial "heavenly crime," the theft of fire from the gods. It is in the word that this fire becomes manifest and it is through the word that the individual realizes the possibility of liberation—the possibility of ecstasy and of the infinite. Like Prometheus, Huidobro too creates his new human "looking into the stars." To read one of his poems is to pass through the sky. It is to pass through a landscape filled with planets and birds, with feathers, comets and angels, with the beating wings of the poet in flight, the poet on his epic voyage.

> The hero is an unrealized God, or rather the concept of God, our desire for God. Our desire for the absolute made flesh.

Huidobro—not unlike Rimbaud whom he greatly admired—attempted to become this new culture hero through both his poetry and the *mythos* he surrounded it with. He claimed to be the last living descendant of the Cid and actually rewrote the great adventurer's history in *Mío Cid Campeador*. He wrote too of Columbus, Napoleon, Cagliostro, Don Juan, and Joan of Arc, believing himself to be their heir in the greatest quest of all—that of the infinite and the new language which would liberate it.

Finally, he created Altazor, the personification of the Promethean hero:*

The double of myself
The one who sees himself working and laughs at the other face to face
The one who fell from the heights of his star
And travelled for twenty-five years
Loaded with the parachutes of his own prejudices
I am Altazor of the infinite desire
Of the hunger eternal and unsatisfied
With flesh tilled by the plows of grief
How can I rest with unknown worlds inside?

Altazor is Huidobro's great epic and one of the most important poems in the Spanish language. It is, as the Chilean poet Enrique Lihn has written, Huidobro's "Song of Myself." Through Cubist objectivism, Huidobro had been liberated from the breast-beating sentimentality which had come to weigh down so much of Latin American and Spanish literature. Through a reordering of the image and a reorganization of the line, he had been able to create startling and beautiful "new worlds," worlds where the "emotion is born from the creative strength alone." In *Poemas Articos,* he had written:

With a shout I made a mountain rise
And now we do a new dance around it

But the mountain was not high enough. A more total vision was still required. The poet and the word were still "moored." His last two books in French, *Automne Régulier* and *Tout A Coup* are filled with

* The name Altazor is actually a word compound formed from *alto*-high and *azor*-hawk.

foretellings of the eruption about to take place, foretellings of the "universe coming loose." And so, as if to reject the world that had shaped his poetry so thoroughly, he gave up its language and returned to Spanish. The Cubist tradition which had once freed him had by now become constrictive. Nonreferential poetry, calligrams, mixed typography, lack of punctuation, imagery that "unglued the moon" had all been revolutionary, but in the end, were not enough to achieve the language of power and revelation which Huidobro ultimately sought.

It is in *Altazor* that Huidobro achieved his true poetry of "transubstantiation." It is here that he becomes the true visionary poet "measuring the infinite step by step." Here is "the unexplored ground" and the word made flesh. Here is the world recreated through the word, and language recreated through the ecstatic vision of the poet. And here is the poet in flight, the poet "in parachutes": the poet "falling to the very bottom of himself" "to break all the chains."

Altazor, subtitled *The Parachute Voyage,* was begun in 1919 and published in Madrid in 1931. The first edition ran 111 pages and included a preface and seven cantos. In it, the poet continues the journey begun in *Poemas Articos* and *Ecuatorial.* Language and the word itself are systematically reconstructed. The process is careful and clear, the poet's voyage fastidiously described. The voyage, once again, the ultimate Creationist one from "man-mirror to man-God." In the middle of the poem sits the windmill, physical presence of the transformation of consciousness and language. It is through this mill—the ancient symbol of Cervantes—that all language (and prejudice) must pass to be ground and recreated: "And wheat comes and goes, from earth to heaven."

The mill becomes a mantra. "The poet goes into a trance of communication with the universe" and the universe speaks through him:

> Here and now I have to dilute myself into many things
> I am firefly and I go lighting the boughs of the forest
> However when I fly I watch the way I move
> And I'm not only firefly
> But also the air it flies in
> Two birds are lost in my breast
> There's no way to change it
> And soon I'm tree

And with regard to tree I keep my firefly ways
And my sky ways
And my human movement my sad walking
And now I'm a rosebush and speak in rosebush language
And I say
Rise rose rorosarose
Rise rose to the day . . .

And then I'm bird
And I argue all day in chirps
The day the throat crosses me
I alone will speak
Be quiet I'm going to sing
I am the only singer of this age
Mine mine is all the infinite

Poet becomes creation itself, bursting through the "last horizon," past death, with the "keys to the infinite" gripped tightly in his hand.

Altazor ends with the scream of the poet in full flight—consciousness hurtling at the speed of light. The final canto is untranslatable. The roots of some of the words can be traced but they are predominantly the vocables of revelation.

Altazor is Huidobro's most famous work, but it is only a stop on the long journey from *Ecos del Alma* to *Ultimos Poemas*. To read through this great body of work is to witness a poet giving birth to himself. Inside the avant-garde artist who talks of "pure poetry" is the one forever moving inward, the one "tapping his own roots." Inside the ever present metaphor of outer exploration and the exhortations of "ONWARD" is the "endless traveller" on the road to the inner world. "The one with flesh falling off on all sides." The one peeling off mask after mask. The one "in other objects." The animist, looking for God in trees and waves. The "magician" imploring us to fly with him. The "antipoet" giving us a new language. The one of the endless hunger "to be the first free man, the first to break all the chains."

David M. Guss
Berkeley, 1976

A flock of vultures hovers in the air infesting our sky.

Maybe Chile's a giant animal, stretched across the slopes of the Andes, dead.

Shake yourself, my country. Wake up from your long agony and roar. Roar so loud the vultures will flee in terror.

Huidobro, 1925

Prelude

ARTE POETICA

Que el verso sea como una llave
Que abra mil puertas.
Una hoja cae; algo pasa volando;
Cuanto miren los ojos creado sea,
Y el alma del oyente quede temblando.

Inventa mundos nuevos y cuida tu palabra;
El adjetivo, cuando no da vida, mata.

Estamos en el ciclo de los nervios.
El músculo cuelga,
Como recuerdo, en los museos;
Mas no por eso tenemos menos fuerza:
El vigor verdadero
Reside en la cabeza.

Por qué cantáis la rosa, ¡oh Poetas!
Hacedla florecer en el poema;

Sólo para nosotros
Viven todas las cosas bajo el Sol.

El poeta es un pequeño Dios.

de El Espejo de Aqua, *1916*

ARS POETICA

Let poetry be like a key
Opening a thousand doors.
A leaf falls; something flies by;
Let all the eye sees be created
And the soul of the listener tremble.

Invent new worlds and watch your word;
The adjective, when it doesn't give life, kills it.

We are in the age of nerves.
The muscle hangs,
Like a memory, in museums;
But we are not the weaker for it:
True vigor
Resides in the head.

Oh Poets, why sing of roses!
Let them flower in your poems;

For us alone
Do all things live beneath the Sun.

The poet is a little God.   [D.M.G.]

From The Mirror of Water, *1916*

3

from "CREATIONISM"

At the end of 1916 I landed in Paris, into the world of the magazine *Sic*. I barely knew the language, but soon realized that I was dealing with a very futurist scene and one can't forget that just two years before, in my book *Pasando y pasando,* I had attacked futurism as being too old-fashioned, at the exact moment the whole world was crying out for the birth of something completely new.

I searched everywhere for this created poetry, without relation to the external world, and, when at times I believed I had found it, I soon realized that it was merely my lack of knowledge of the language which had made me see it where it was totally lacking or simply existed in small fragments, as in my earlier books of 1913 and 1915.

Have you noticed the special power, the near-creative sense that pervades the poetry written in a language you are just beginning to utter?

You find fantastic poems which just a year later make you smile.

Gathered around Apollinaire, who was such an undeniable poet, and yet apart from him, one found several earnest searchers; unfortunately, most of them lacked the holy fire, since nothing could be more false than to believe that inspiration is to be found lying in the street. True poetic inspiration is the rarest thing that exists. And I'm not using the word poet here in the intimate sense it holds for me, but rather in its habitual sense, since, for me, there has never been a single poet in the history of the planet.

Today I affirm completely, as I did ten years ago in the Atheneum in Buenos Aires: "There has never been a single poem written in the world, but only some vague essays on how to write one. Poetry is yet to be born on our globe. And its birth will be an event that will revolutionize mankind like the greatest earthquake." I sometimes wonder if it will not go by unnoticed.

Let's make it clear, then, that each time I speak of "poet" I simply use the term to be understood, like stretching a rubberband to encircle those who are nearest the importance which I assign it.

During the period of the magazine *Nord-Sud,* of which I was one of the founders, we all had more or less the same orientation in our outlooks, but were far enough from one another at the core.

While others were making oval skylights, I was making square horizons. As all skylights are oval, poetry continues to be realist. As horizons are not square, the author offers something created by himself. When *Horizon Carré* (*Square Horizon*) came out, here is how I explained the title in a letter to friend and critic Thomas Chazal:

Square horizon. A new fact, invented by me, created by me, which couldn't exist without me. I want, my dear friend, to capture in this title the whole of my aesthetics, which you have been aware of for some time now.

This title explains the basis of my poetic theory. Condensed within it is the essence of my principles.

1. To humanize the object. Everything that passes through the body of the poet must be subjected to the greatest possible amount of his heat. Here something as vast and enormous as the horizon is humanized; it becomes intimate, thanks to the adjective SQUARE. The infinite nests in our heart.

2. The indefinite becomes precise. In shutting the windows of our soul, whatever was able to escape, gasify, and unravel, remains enclosed and is solidified.

3. The abstract becomes concrete and the concrete abstract. This means the perfect balance, since if the abstract leaned toward the more abstract, it would dissolve in your hands or filter through your fingers. And if you made the concrete even more concrete, it would help you drink wine or furnish your home, but it would never furnish your soul.

4. Whatever is too poetic to be created is transformed into something created by changing its common value, so that if horizon was poetic in itself, if horizon was poetry in life, by qualifying it with square, it stops being poetry in art. From dead poetry it becomes living poetry.

The few words explaining my concept of poetry on the first page of the book we are speaking of, tells you what I wanted to accomplish in those poems. It said:

To create a poem by taking the elements of life and transforming them to give them a new and independent life of their own.

Nothing descriptive or anecdotal. Emotion must be born from the creative strength alone.

Make a POEM like nature makes a tree.

In the end, it was my exact concept before arriving in Paris: the act of pure creation which you will find, as a true obsession, in every aspect of my work from 1912 on. And this is still my concept of poetry. The poem created in all its parts, as a new object.

I will repeat here the axiom I gave in my talk at the Atheneum in Madrid in 1921, and finally in Paris, in my speech at the Sorbonne, an axiom which sums up my aesthetic principles: "Art is one thing and Nature another. I love Art very much and Nature very much. And if I accept the representations that a man makes from Nature, it proves I love neither Nature or Art."

In two words and to conclude: the creationists are the first poets who have brought to art a poem invented in all its parts by the author.

Here, in these pages about creationism, is my poetic testament. I bequeath it to the poets of tomorrow, to those who will be the first of this new species being, the poet, this new species to be born soon; I can feel it. There are signs in the sky.

The near-poets of today are very interesting, but their interests do not interest me.

The wind points my flute toward the future.   [D.M.G.]

from Manifestos, *1925*

6

Horizon Carré

Square Horizon

1917

NOUVELLE CHANSON POUR TOI, MANUELITA

En dedans de l'Horizon
QUELQU'UN CHANTAIT

Sa voix
N'est pas connue

D'OU VIENT-IL

Parmi les branches
On ne voit personne

La lune même était une oreille

Et on n'entend
aucun bruit

Cependant
une étoile déclouée

Est tombée dans l'étang

L'HORIZON
S'EST FERME

Et il n'y a pas de sortie

ORAGE   A MAX JACOB

Nuit de tempête
L'obscurité me mord la tête

Les diables
cochers du tonnerre
sont en vacances

Personne ne passe dans la rue
Elle n'est pas venue

Quelque chose
est tombé dans le coin
Et la pendule
ne bouge plus

NEW SONG

FOR YOU, MANUELITA

Inside the horizon
SOMEONE WAS SINGING

        The voice
      Is unfamiliar

          WHERE IS IT COMING FROM

No one can be seen
Among the branches

Even the moon was an ear

And not a sound
        is heard

     Yet

         a loose star

Fell in the pond

    THE HORIZON
        IS CLOSED

And there is no exit   [G.O.]

STORM

FOR MAX JACOB

Stormy night
The darkness bites my head

The devils
    who drive the thunder
              are having their vacation

No one goes by in the street
She hasn't come

Something
      fell in the corner
And the clock
      stopped

Parfois le trolley
VILLE Fait s'envoler
de petits oiseaux de feu
Dans la montagne
Les troupeaux
CAMPAGNE
tremblent sous l'orage

Le chien boîteux qui surveille
Cherche son ombre

Viens plus près de moi
On fera un beau voyage

Dans le désert de l'Afrique
Les girafes veulent avaler la lune
Il ne faut pas regarder
derrière les murs
La curiosité allonge les cous

On se cherche
Et l'on ne trouve pas le chemin

Je cache un souvenir
Mais c'est inutile de regarder mes yeux

Autour de la maison
le vent gronde

Peut-être là-bas ma mère
pleure

UN COUP DE TONNERRE FATIGUE

S'est posé sur le plus haut sommet

TELEPHONE

FILS TELEPHONIQUES
CHEMIN DES MOTS

Et dans la nuit
Violon de la lune

UNE VOIX

At moments the trolley
CITY Lets fly
   little birds of fire
On the mountain   COUNTRY
The flocks
  tremble in the storm

The crippled watchdog
Looks for his shadow

    Come closer to me
    We'll go on a beautiful trip

In the African desert
    The giraffes want to swallow the moon
You mustn't look
    behind walls
Curiosity will make your neck long

   Someone tries to see where he is
   And doesn't find the road

I'm hiding a memory
But it's useless to look in my eyes

Around the house
   the wind growls

Maybe down there my mother
     is crying

A TIRED THUNDERCLAP

  Landed on the highest peak   [G.O.]

TELEPHONE

TELEPHONE WIRES
PATH OF WORDS

   And in the night
   The moon's violin

    A VOICE

Une montagne
             s'est levée devant moi
Ce qui attend derrière
                     cherche son chemin

DEUX ENDROITS
                     DEUX OREILLES

    Une route longue à parcourir

Paroles
        le long de ton cheveu
Une est tombée à l'eau

ALLO
                                 ALLO

C H A N S O N

Quelqu'un
            que tu n'es pas
Chante derrière le mur

Le miroir
          dédoublait la voix
Et des étoiles naufragées
                     Dormaient sur tes seins

QUI ES-TU

                     La voix qui a répondu
Venait de plus loin que ta poitrine

A mountain
                    rose up in front of me
What waits in back of me
                              is looking for the right road

TWO PLACES

                              TWO EARS

        A long way to go

Words
        all the length of your hair
One of them fell in the water below

HELLO

                              HELLO
                                    [G.O.]

SONG

Someone
            that you aren't
Is singing behind the wall
The mirror
                split the voice in half
And shipwrecked stars
                        Slept on your breasts

WHO ARE YOU

                    The voice that answered
Came from farther off than your chest   [G.O.]

COW-BOY
à Jacques Lipschitz

Sur le Far West
    où il y a une seule lune
Le Cok Boy chante
    à rompre la nuit
Et son cigare est une étoile
      filante
SON POULAIN FERRÉ D'AILES
    N'A JAMAIS EU DE PANNE
Et lui
    la tête contre les genoux
      danse un Cake Walk
  New York
    à quelques kilomtères
Dans les gratte-ciels
Les ascenseurs montent comme des thermomètres
Et près du Niagara
      qui a éteint ma pipe
Je regarde les étoiles éclaboussées
Le Cow Boy
     sur une corde à violon
  Traverse l'Ohio

Vincente HUIDOBRO

H. ARP

Reproduced from Tristan Tzara's *Dada 3,* Zurich,
1918, woodcut by Hans Arp.

C O W   B O Y

In the Far West
                    where there is only one moon
The Cok Boy sings
                    until it breaks the night
And his cigar is a wandering star

        HIS PONY SHOED WITH WINGS
        HAS NEVER HAD A FLAW

And him
            his head against his knees
                            he dances a Cake Walk

New York
            a few kilometers

In the skyscrapers
The elevators rise like thermometers

And near Niagara
                    which has put out my pipe
I watch the spattered stars

The Cow Boy
            on a violin string
Crosses the Ohio   [D.M.G.]

15

Tour Eiffel

Eiffel Tower

1918

TOUR EIFFEL

A ROBERT DELAUNAY

Tour Eiffel
Guitare du ciel

    Ta télégraphie sans fil
    Attire les mots
    Comme un rosier les abeilles

Pendant la nuit
La Seine ne coule plus

    Télescope ou clairon

    TOUR EIFFEL

Et c'est une ruche de mots
Ou un encrier de miel

Au fond de l'aube
Une araignée aux pattes en fil de fer
Faisait sa toile de nuages

    Mon petit garçon
    Pour monter à la Tour Eiffel
    On monte sur une chanson

    Do
      ré
        mi
          fa
            sol
              la
                si
                  do

    Nous sommes en haut

Un oiseau chante   C'est le vent
Dans les antennes   De l'Europe
Télégraphiques   Le vent électrique

    Là-bas

Les chapeaux s'envolent
Ils ont des ailes mais ils ne chantent pas

EIFFEL TOWER

FOR ROBERT DELAUNAY

Eiffel Tower
The sky's guitar

> Words are drawn
> To your wireless telegraphy
> Like bees to a rose-bush

During the night
The Seine stops flowing

> Telescope or bugle

> EIFFEL TOWER

And it's a hive of words
Or an inkwell of honey

At the far end of dawn
A spider with steel-wire legs
Made its web of clouds

> My little boy
> To climb the Eiffel Tower
> You climb up on a song

> Do
>   re
>   mi
>   fa
>   so
>   la
>   ti
>   do

> We're up on top

A bird sings   It is the wind
In the telegraph   Of Europe
Antennas   The electric wind

> Down there

The hats take flight
They have wings but don't sing

Jacqueline
>> Fille de France
Qu'est-ce que tu vois là-haut

La Seine dort
Sous l'ombre de ses ponts

Je vois tourner la Terre
Et je sonne mon clairon
Vers toutes les mers

>> Sur le chemin
>> De ton parfum
>> Tous les abeilles et les paroles s'en vont

>> Sur les quatre horizons
Qui n'a pas entendu cette chanson

JE SUIS LA REINE DE L'AUBE DES POLES
JE SUIS LA ROSE DES VENTS QUI SE FANE TOUS LES
>> AUTOMNES
ET TOUTE PLEINE DE NEIGE
JE MEURS DE LA MORT DE CETTE ROSE
DANS MA TETE UN OISEAU CHANTE TOUTE L'ANNEE

C'est comme ça qu'un jour la Tour m'a parlé

Tour Eiffel
>> Volière du monde
>>>> Chante   Chante

Sonnerie de Paris

Le géant pendu au milieu du vide
Est l'affiche de France

>>>> Le jour de la Victoire
>>>> Tu la raconteras aux étoiles

Jacqueline
            Daughter of France
What do you see up there

The Seine is sleeping
Under the shadow of its bridges

I see the Earth turn
And I blow my bugle
Toward every ocean

            All the bees and all the words take off
            Along the path
            Of your perfume

            On the four horizons
Who has not heard this song

I AM THE QUEEN OF THE DAWN OF THE POLES
I AM THE ROSE OF THE WINDS THAT FADES EVERY AUTUMN
AND FILLED WITH SNOW
I DIE OF THE DEATH OF THAT ROSE
INSIDE MY HEAD A BIRD SINGS ALL YEAR LONG

That's the way the Tower spoke to me one day

Eiffel Tower
Aviary of the world
            Sing   Sing

Paris fanfare

The giant hanging in the midst of the void
Is an advertisement for France
                        On the day of Victory
                        You'll tell it to the stars

                                    [G.O.]

Ecuatorial

Equatorial

1918

ECUATORIAL

A PABLO PICASSO

Era el tiempo en que se abrieron mis párpados sin alas
Y empecé a cantar sobre las lejanías desatadas

Saliendo de sus nidos
            Atruenan el aire las banderas

LOS HOMBRES
         ENTRE LA YERBA
                BUSCABAN LAS FRONTERAS

Sobre el campo banal
         el mundo muere
De las cabezas prematuras
            brotan alas ardientes
Y en la trinchera ecuatorial
            trizada a trechos
Bajo la sombra de aeroplanos vivos
Los soldados cantaban en las tardes duras

Las ciudades de Europa
         se apagan una a una

Caminando al destierro
El último rey portaba al cuello
Una cadena de lámparas extintas

      Las estrellas
          que caían
      Eran luciérnagas del musgo

Y los afiches ahorcados
            pendían a lo largo de los muros

Una sombra rodó sobre la falda de los montes
Donde el viejo organista hace cantar las selvas

      El viento mece los horizontes
      Colgados de las jarcias y las velas

Sobre el arco iris
        un pájaro cantaba

      Abridme la montaña

EQUATORIAL

FOR PABLO PICASSO

It was the time when my eyelids opened without wings
And I began to sing above unleashed distances

Going out from their nests

                Flags shatter the air

THE MEN

      IN THE GRASS

            WERE LOOKING FOR BORDERS

On the ugly field

        the world is dying
From the unripe heads

           burning wings sprout
And in the equatorial trench

           shattered at intervals
Beneath the shadow of moving aeroplanes
The soldiers were singing in the unbearable afternoons

The cities of Europe

        go out one by one

Walking into exile
The last king was carrying a chain
Of extinct lamps around his neck

        The stars
          which fell
        Were glowworms of moss

And by their necks the notices

        were dangling along the walls

A shadow circled above the foothills
Where the ancient organist makes the trees sing

        Wind tosses the horizons
        Suspended by tackle and sails

Above the rainbow

        a bird was singing

        Open the mountain

Por todas partes en el suelo
He visto alas de golondrinas
Y el Cristo que alzó el vuelo
Dejó olvidada la corona de espinas

    Sentados sobre el paralelo
    Miremos nuestro tiempo

SIGLO ENCADENADO EN UN ANGULO DEL MUNDO

En los espejos corrientes
Pasan las barcas bajo los puentes
Y los ángeles-correo
      reposan en el humo de los dreadnoughts

Entre la hierba
    silba la locomotora en celo
Que atravesó el invierno

Las dos cuerdas de su rastro
Tras ella quedan cantando
Como una guitarra indócil

Su ojo desnudo
    Cigarro del horizonte
        Danza entre los árboles

Ella es el Diógenes con la pipa encendida
Buscando entre los meses y los días

Sobre el sendero equinoccial
Empecé a caminar

Cada estrella
    es un obús que estalla

Las plumas de mi garganta
Se entibiaron al sol
    que perdió un ala

El divino aeroplano
Traía un ramo de olivo entre las manos

Sin embargo
    Los ocasos heridos se desangran

Everywhere on earth
I have seen wings of swallows
And Christ who took off in flight
Forgot his crown of thorns

Seated above the parallel
Let us look at our age

CENTURY CHAINED TO A CORNER OF THE WORLD

In the floating mirrors
The boats pass beneath the bridges
And the mail-angels
                rest in the dreadnoughts' smoke

In the grass
          the locomotive that crossed the winter
Whistles in heat

Behind it
The two strings of its track keep singing
Like a wild guitar

Its naked eye
        Cigar of the horizon
                Dances through the trees

It is Diogenes with tub inflamed
Searching among the months and days

Upon the equinoctial path
I start to travel

Each star
        is a bursting shell

The feathers of my throat
Were fanned by the sun
           which lost a wing

The divine aeroplane
Brought an olive branch in its hands

But
    The wounded sunsets still bleed

Y en el puerto los días que se alejan
Llevaban una cruz en el sitio del ancla

Cantando nos sentamos en las playas

Los más bravos capitanes   El capitán Cook
En un iceberg iban a los polos   Caza auroras boreales
Para dejar su pipa en labios   En el Polo Sur
Esquimales

Otros clavan frescas lanzas en el Congo

El corazón del Africa soleado
Se abre como los higos picoteados

Y los negros
            de divina raza
Esclavos en Europa
Limpiaban de su rostro
                    la nieve que los mancha

Hombre de alas cortas
                    han recorrido todo
Y un noble explorador de la Noruega
Como botín de guerra
Trajo a Europa
            entre raros animales
Y árboles exóticos
Los cuatro puntos cardinales

Yo he embarcado también
Dejando mi arrecife vine a veros

Las gaviotas volaban en torno a mi sombrero

Y heme aquí
        de pie
            en otras bahías

Bajo el boscaje afónico
Pasan lentamente
                las ciudades cautivas
Cosidas una a una por hilos telefónicos

Y las palabras y los gestos
Vuelan en torno del telégrafo

And in the harbor the days move off
Carrying crosses in place of anchors

Singing we settle on the beaches

The bravest captains	Captain Cook
Were leaving on an iceberg	Is chasing aurora borealises
For the poles to plant	In the South Pole
Their pipe in Eskimo lips	

Others plant new spears in the Congo

The bleached heart of Africa
Opens like chopped figs

And blacks
              of the divine race
Slaves in Europe
Were washing from their face
                            the snow which stains them

Men with short wings
                        have overrun everything
And a noble explorer from Norway
Like war booty
Brought to Europe
                    among rare animals
And exotic plants
The four cardinal points

I too have embarked
Leaving my reef I came to see you

Sea gulls flew around my hat

And here I am
              on foot
                      in other bays

Beneath the silent woods
The captive cities
                    slowly pass
Sewn to one another by telephone wires

And words and faces
Fly around the telegraph

Quemándose las alas
                    cual dioses inexpertos
Los aeroplanos fatigados
Iban a posarse sobre los pararrayos

Biplanos encintas
                    pariendo al vuelo entre la niebla

Son los pájaros amados
Que en nuestras jaulas han cantado

Es el pájaro que duerme entre las ramas
Sin cubrir la cabeza bajo el ala

En las noches
                    los aviones volaban junto al faro
El faro que agoniza al fondo de los años

Alguien amargado
                    Las pupilas vacías
Lanzando al mar sus tristes días
Toma el barco

Partir
        Y de allá lejos
Mirar las ventanas encendidas
Y las sombras que cruzan los espejos

Como una bandada
                    de golondrinas jóvenes
Los emigrantes cantaban sobre las olas invertidas

MAR

MAR DE HUMAREDAS VERDES

Yo querría ese mar para mi sed de antaño

Lleno de flotantes cabelleras

Sobre esas olas fuéronse mis ansias verdaderas

Bajo las aguas gaseosas
                    Un serafín náufrago
                    Teje coronas de algas

Singeing their wings
                    like inept gods

Tired aeroplanes
Were leaving to rest on lightning rods

Biplanes in labor
                    laying eggs in flight among the mist

They are the love birds
That sung in our cages

It is the bird that sleeps in the branches
But doesn't cover its head beneath its wing

At night
                    the planes flew by the lighthouse
The lighthouse which dies at the end of its years

Someone embittered
                    His empty pupils
Casting their gloomy daylight into the sea
Takes the boat

To leave
                    And then from far away
To watch the windows burning
And the shadows crossing the mirrors

Like a flock
                    of young swallows
The emigrants were singing above the inverted waves

SEA

SEA OF GREEN MYSTERIES

I cherished that sea for my ancient thirst

Filled with strands of floating hair

Over those waves my real desires flew

Beneath the gaseous waters
                    A shipwrecked angel
                    Weaves crowns of seaweed

La luna nueva
                con las jarcias rotas
Ancló en Marsella esta mañana

Y los más viejos marineros
En el fondo del humo de sus pipas
Habían encontrado perlas vivas

El capitán del submarino
Olvidó en el fondo su destino

Al volver a la tierra
                vio que otro llevaba su estrella

Desterrados fiebrosos del planeta viejo
Muerto al alzar el vuelo
Por los cañones antiaéreos

Un emigrante ciego
                traía cuatro leones maestrados
Y otro llevaba al hospital del puerto
Un ruiseñor desafinado

Aquel piloto niño
                que olvidó su pipa humeante
Junto al volcán extinto
Encontró en la ciudad
                los hombres de rodillas
Y vio alumbrar las vírgenes encintas

Allá lejos

                                                    Allá lejos

Vienen pensativos
                los buscadores de oro
Pasan cantando entre las hojas
Sobre sus hombros
Traen la California

Al fondo del crepúsculo
Venían los mendigos semimudos

Un rezador murmullo
                inclinaba los árboles

The new moon
                with its rigging battered
Anchored in Marseilles this morning

And the oldest sailors
Have found pearls shining
At the bottom of their pipes' smoke

In the depths
The submarine captain forgot his mission

On returning to land
                he saw that someone else was holding his star

Feverish exiles from the ancient planet
Killed by antiaircraft guns
In a flying disaster

A blind emigrant
                was leading four trained lions
And from the port another was carrying
An out-of-tune nightingale to the hospital

That young pilot
                who forgot his smoking pipe
Near the extinct volcano
Found men on their knees
                in the city
And saw pregnant virgins giving birth

Over there in the distance

                                        Over there far off

The gold seekers are coming
                deep in thought
They walk through the leaves singing
Upon their shoulders
They carry California

In the depths of the twilight
The half-dumb beggars came

A whispering supplicant
                was bending the trees

Sobre los mares
Huyó el estío

QUE DE COSAS HE VISTO

Entre la niebla vegetal y espesa
Los mendigos de las calles de Londres
Pegados como anuncios
Contra los fríos muros

Recuerdo bien
    Recuerdo

Aquella tarde en primavera
Una muchacha enferma
Dejando sus dos alas a la puerta
Entraba al sanatorio

Aquella misma noche
      bajo el cielo oblongo
Diez Zeppelines vinieron a París
Y un cazador de jabalís
Dejó sangrando siete
Sobre el alba agreste

Entre la nube que rozaba el techo
Un reloj verde
     Anuncia el año

      1917

LLUEVE

       Bajo el agua
       Enterraban los muertos
    Alguien que lloraba
    Hacía caer las hojas

Signos hay en el cielo
Dice el astrólogo barbudo
     Una manzana y una estrella
     Picotean los búhos

Marte
  pasa a través de
     Sagitario

Over the seas
Summer fled

WHAT THINGS I HAVE SEEN

In the thick vegetal fog
The street beggars of London
Clung like posters
To the cold walls

I remember exactly
                    I remember

That afternoon in spring
A sick woman
Leaving her two wings by the door
Was entering the sanatorium

That same night
                    beneath the oblong sky
Ten Zeppelins arrived in Paris
And a hunter of wild boars
Left seven bleeding
Above the wild dawn

Inside the cloud that scraped the roof

A green clock
                    Announces the year

                    1917

IT'S RAINING

                              Beneath the water
                              They were burying the dead
                    Someone who was crying
                    Made the leaves fall

There are signs in the sky
Says the bearded astrologer
                              Owls peck
                              An apple and a star

Mars
            passes through
                              Sagittarius

SALE LA LUNA

Un astro maltratado
Se desliza

Astrólogos de mitras puntiagudas
De sus barbas caían copos de ceniza

Y heme aquí
entre las selvas afinadas
Más sabiamente que las viejas arpas

En la casa
que cuelga del vacío
Cansados de buscar
los Reyes Magos se han dormido

Los ascensores descansan en cuclillas

Y en todas las alcobas
Cada vez que da la hora
Salía del reloj un paje serio
Como a decir
El coche aguarda
mi señora

Junto a la puerta viva
El negro esclavo
abre la boca prestamente
Para el amo pianista
Que hace cantar sus dientes

Esta tarde yo he visto
Los últimos afiches fonográficos
Era una confusión de gritos
Y cantos tan diversos
Como en los puertos extranjeros

Los hombres de mañana
Vendrán a descifrar los jeroglíficos
Que dejamos ahora
Escritos al revés
Entre los hierros de la Torre Eiffel

THE MOON COMES UP

                    A mistreated star
                    Glides away

Snowflakes of ash were falling from the beards
Of the pointy-mitered astrologers

And here I am
                    in woods kept
More wisely than the ancient harps

In the house
                    which hangs from space
Tired from searching
                    the Magi have gone to sleep

The elevators rest in a squatting position

And in every bedroom
Each time the hour strikes
A dignified valet steps out of the clock
As if to say
                    Your car is waiting
                                        my lady

Near the swinging door
The black slave
                    quickly opens his mouth
For the pianist lord
Who makes his teeth sing

This afternoon I saw
The latest phonographic presses
It was a maze of screams
And songs as varied
As in foreign ports

Tomorrow's men
Will come to decipher the hieroglyphics
We leave today
Written in reverse
On the girders of the Eiffel Tower

Llegamos al final de la refriega
Mi reloj perdió todas sus horas

Yo te recorro lentamente
Siglo cortado en dos
                    Y con un puente
Sobre un río sangriento
Camino de Occidente

Una tarde
            al fondo de la vida
Pasaba un horizonte de camellos
En sus espaldas mudas
Entre dos pirámides huesudas
Los hombres del Egipto
Lloran como los nuevos cocodrilos

Y los santos en tren
                    buscando otras regiones
Bajaban y subían en todas las estaciones

Mi alma hermana de los trenes

                Un tren puede rezarse como un rosario
                La cruz humeante perfumaba los llanos

Henos aquí viajando entre los santos

El tren es un trozo de la ciudad que se aleja

El anunciador de estaciones
Ha gritado
                        Primavera
                        Al lado izquierdo
                        30 minutos

Pasa el tren lleno de flores y de frutos

El Niágara ha mojado mis cabellos
Y una neblina nace en torno de ellos

Los ríos
            Todos los ríos de las nacientes cabelleras
Los ríos mal trenzados
Que los ardientes veranos han besado

We reached the battle's end
My watch lost all its time

I slowly cross over you
Age cut in two
              And by a bridge
Over a bloody river
I travel West

One afternoon
              in the heat of life
I passed a horizon of camels
On their silent backs
Between two bony pyramids
Egyptian men
Weep like newborn crocodiles

And on the train the saints

                                searching for other regions

Get off and on at every station

My soul sister of the trains

          A train can pray like a rosary
           The smoking cross scented the plains

Here we are travelling among saints

The train is a piece of the city which fades away

The stationmaster
Yelled

                 Spring
                 On the left
                 30 minutes

The train passes full of flowers and fruits

Niagara has wet my hair
And a mist is forming around it

Rivers
       All the rivers with their floating hair
Rivers poorly braided
Which the burning summers have kissed

Un paquebot perdido costeaba
Las islas de oro de la Vía Láctea

La cordillera Andina
                    Veloz como un convoy
Atraviesa la América Latina

El Amor

                                                            El Amor

En pocos sitios lo he encontrado
Y todos los ríos no explorados
Bajo mis brazos han pasado

Una mañana
                Pastores alpinistas
Tocaban el violín sobre la Suiza

Y en la estrella vecina
Aquel que no tenía manos
Con las alas tocaba el piano

Siglo embarcado en aeroplanos ebrios

                        A DONDE IRAS

Caminando al destierro
El último rey portaba al cuello
Una cadena de lámparas extintas

Y ayer vi muerta entre las rosas
La amatista de Roma

ALFA

                                    OMEGA

                DILUVIO

                                            ARCO IRIS

Cuántas veces la vida habrá recomenzado

Quién dirá todo lo que en un astro ha pasado

                Sigamos nuestra marcha
                Llevando la cabeza madura entre las manos

EL RUISEÑOR MECANICO HA CANTADO

A lost steamer was coasting
The golden islands off the Milky Way

The Andes
              Swift as a convoy
Run across Latin America

Love

                                        Love

In so few places have I found you
And every unexplored river
Has passed beneath my arms

One morning
              Alpinist shepherds
Were playing the violin over Switzerland

And in the neighboring star
The one who had no hands
Was playing the piano with wings

Century embarked on drunken aeroplanes

                    WHERE WILL YOU GO

Walking into exile
The last king was carrying a chain
Of extinct lamps around his neck

And yesterday I saw the Roman amethyst
Dead among the roses

ALPHA

                                        OMEGA

                    FLOOD

                                                  RAINBOW

How many times will life have begun again

Who will tell everything that has happened on a star

                    Let's be on our way
                    Taking the ripe head in our hands

THE MECHANICAL NIGHTINGALE HAS SUNG

Aquella multitud de manos ásperas
Lleva coronas funerarias
Hacia los campos de batalla

Alguien pasó perdido en su cigarro

QUIEN ES

Una mano cortada
Dejó sobre los mármoles
La línea ecuatorial recién brotada

Siglo
            Sumérgete en el sol
Cuando en la tarde
            Aterrice en un campo de aviación

Hacia el solo aeroplano
Que cantará un día en el azul
Se alzará de los años
Una bandada de manos

CRUZ DEL SUR

SUPREMO SIGNO   AVION DE CRISTO

El niño sonrosado de las alas desnudas
Vendrá con el clarín entre los dedos
El clarín aún fresco que anuncia
El Fin del Universo

That multitude of rough hands
Carries funeral wreaths
Toward the battlefields

Someone passed lost in his cigar

WHO IS IT

Over the marbles
An amputated hand dropped
The equatorial line just sprouted

Time
Drown yourself in the sun
As it lands on an airfield
In the afternoon

Near the lone plane
Which will sing in the blue one day
A flock of hands
Will rise from the years

SOUTHERN CROSS

SUPREME SIGN   PLANE OF CHRIST

The child blushing with naked wings
Will come with the horn between his fingers
The horn still calm that blows
The End of the World   [D.M.G.]

Poemas Articos

Arctic Poems

1918

EXPRES

Una corona yo me haría
De todas las ciudades recorridas

    Londres   Madrid   París
    Roma   Nápoles Zurich

Silban en los llanos
               locomotoras cubiertas de algas

      AQUI NADIE HE ENCONTRADO

De todos los ríos navegados
yo me haría un collar

    El Amazonas   El Sena
    El Támesis   El Rin

Cien embarcaciones sabias
Que han plegado las alas

      Y mi canción de marinero huérfano
      Diciendo adiós a las playas

Aspirar el aroma del Monte Rosa
Trenzar las canas errantes del Monte Blanco
Y sobre el cenit del Monte Cenis
Encender en el sol muriente
El último cigarro

Un silbido horada el aire

      No es un juego de agua

      ADELANTE

Apeninos gibosos
      marchan hacia el desierto

Las estrellas del oasis
Nos darán miel de sus dátiles

En la montaña
El viento hace crujir las jarcias
Y todos los montes dominados

EXPRESS

I would make a crown
Of all the cities I have known

London	Madrid	Paris
Rome	Naples	Zurich

Locomotives covered with seaweed

        whistle through the plains

I HAVE FOUND NO ONE HERE

I would make a necklace
From all the rivers I have crossed

The Amazon	The Seine
The Thames	The Rhine

A hundred brilliant ships
That have closed their wings

        And my orphaned sailor's song
        Bidding the shore farewell

To breathe the perfume of Mount Rose
To braid the flowing hair of Mont Blanc
And then on top Mount Summit
To light the last cigar
In the dying sun

A whistle splits the air

        It's not a waterfall

ONWARD

Hunchbacked Apennines

        leave for the desert

The stars of the oasis
Will give us honey from their dates

On the mountain
The wind makes the rigging creak
And all the conquered peaks

Los volcanes bien cargados
Levarán el ancla

ALLA ME ESPERARAN

Buen viaje

Un poco más lejos
Termina la Tierra

Pasan los ríos bajo las barcas
La vida ha de pasar

HASTA MAÑANA

C A M I N O

Un cigarro en el vacío

A lo largo del camino
He deshojado mis dedos

Y jamás mirar atrás

Mi cabellera
Y el humo de esta pipa

Aquella luz me conducía
Todos los pájaros sin alas
En mis hombros cantaron

Pero mi corazón fatigado
Murió en el último nido

Llueve sobre el camino
Y voy buscando el sitio
donde mis lágrimas han caído

E M I G R A N T E   A   A M E R I C A

Estrellas eléctricas
Se encienden en el viento

The volcanoes fully charged
Will lift anchor

THEY'LL BE WAITING FOR ME THERE

Bon voyage

The earth ends
A little further on

SO LONG

Rivers pass beneath the boats
                    Life must pass   [D.M.G.]

ROAD

        A cigar in the void

Along the road
I lost my fingers

                    And never looked back

My long hair
            And the smoke from this pipe

That light was guiding me
All the birds without wings
Sang on my shoulders

                        But my tired heart
                        Died in the last nest

It's raining on the road
And I'm looking for the spot
                        where my tears have fallen
                                            [D.M.G.]

EMIGRANT TO AMERICA

Electric stars
Catch fire in the wind

49

                    Y algunos signos astrológicos
                                        han caído al mar
               Ese emigrante que canta
               Partirá mañana

Vivir
                              Buscar

  Atado al barco
                 como a un horóscopo
  Veinte días sobre el mar

  Bajo las aguas
  Nadan los pulpos vegetales

  Detrás del horizonte abierto
       El otro puerto

  Entre el boscaje
  Las rosas deshojadas
                    iluminan las calles

M A R I N O

  Aquel pájaro que vuela por primera vez
  Se aleja del nido mirando hacia atrás

  Con el dedo en los labios
                    os he llamado

  Yo inventé juegos de agua
  En la cima de los árboles

  Te hice la más bella de las mujeres
  Tan bella que enrojecías en las tardes

              La luna se aleja de nosotros
              Y arroja una corona sobre el polo

  Hice correr ríos
                que nunca han existido

And some astrological signs
have fallen in the sea

That emigrant who's singing
Will leave tomorrow

To live

To search

Tied to the ship
as to a horoscope
Twenty days upon the sea

Beneath the waters
Vegetal octopuses swim

Behind the open horizon
The other port

Among the trees
The stripped roses
light the streets   [D.M.G.]

SAILOR

That bird flying for the first time
Leaves its nest looking back

With a finger to my lips
I called to you

I invented waterfalls
In the tops of trees

I made you the most beautiful woman
So beautiful that you blushed in the evenings

The moon drifts off
And plants a wreath around the pole

I made rivers run
where none had been before

De un grito elevé una montaña
Y en torno bailamos una nueva danza

     Corté todas las rosas
     De las nubes del este

Y enseñé a cantar un pájaro de nieve

Marchemos sobre los meses desatados

Soy el viejo marino
         que cose los horizontes cortados

MARES ARTICOS

Los mares árticos
      Colgados del ocaso

Entre las nubes se quema un pájaro
Día a día
     Las plumas iban cayendo
Sobre las tejas de todos los tejados

Quién ha desenrollado el arco iris

        Ya no hay descanso
      Blando de alas
          Era mi lecho

Sobre los mares árticos
Busco la alondra que voló de mi pecho

With a shout I made a mountain rise
And now we do a new dance around it

                I cut all the roses
                From the clouds of the East

And I taught a snowbird how to sing

Let's depart upon the floating months

I'm the old sailor
               who mends torn horizons   [D.M.G.]

ARCTIC SEAS

Arctic seas
          Suspended from the sunset

Among the clouds a bird is burning
Day after day
            Feathers kept falling
On the tiles of every roof

Who unfurled the rainbow

                 There's no peace now
             My bed was
                   Soft as wings

Across the arctic seas
I search for the lark that flew from my breast

                              [D.M.G.]

Automne Régulier

Ordinary Autumn

1925

AUTOMNE REGULIER

La lune tourne en vain

Dans ma main
La nuit et le jour
Se sont rencontrés
Et l'angle ouvert mieux qu'une bouche
Avale mes pensées

La lune moulin à vent
Tourne tourne tourne en vain
Le paysage au fond des âges
Et l'étang dans sa cage

En vain tu cherches
Arbre d'automne
Il n'y a plus d'oiseaux
     Il n'y a plus d'oiseaux
En regardant sur les vallées
On voit partout des sons de cloches fanés
Le jour est plein mes mains aussi

A l'autre bout s'en sont allés
Les pas sans bruit

C'EST L'AUTOMNE DES CLOCHERS

Je ne sais plus de blonde ou brune
Laissons la place aux matelots
Viens regarder dans mes îlots
La nature morte du clair de lune
Avec l'assiette au bord de l'eau
Et la rose s'effeuillant sur l'oiseau qui chante
A minuit quarante

Oublie-moi
   Petit astre caché
C'est l'heure où j'embaume ma forêt
       Oublie-moi

Pilote sans navire et sans loi

ORDINARY AUTUMN

The moon turns in vain

Night and day
Have met in my hand
And the angle open wider than a mouth
Is swallowing my thoughts

The windmill moon
Turns three times in vain
The landscape at the end of the ages
And the pond in its cage

Tree of autumn
You search in vain
There are no more birds
                           There are no more birds
Gazing across the valleys
Everywhere you see the sound of tarnished bells
Day is full my hands are too

The silent steps have left
By the other exit

IT'S THE BELLTOWERS' AUTUMN

I can't tell blonde from brunette anymore
Let's leave public squares to sailors
Among my islands come and watch
The still life of moonlight with plate
At water's edge
And the rose shedding petals on the bird that sings
At forty past midnight

Forget about me
                  Little hidden star
This is the hour I perfume my forest
                              Forget about me

Pilot with no ship and no laws

Au fond de mes yeux
Chantera toujours le poète noyé

RELATIVITE DU PRINTEMPS

On ne peut rien faire contre les soirs de Mai
Quelquefois la nuit dans les mains se défait
Et je sais que tes yeux sont le fond de la nuit

A huit heures du matin toutes les feuilles sont nées
Au lieu de tant d'étoiles nous en aurons des fruits

Quand on s'en va on ferme le paysage
Et personne n'a soigné les moutons de la plage

Le Printemps est relatif comme l'arc-en-ciel
Il pourrait aussi bien être une ombrelle
Une ombrelle sur un soupir à midi

Le soleil est éteint par la pluie

Ombrelle de la montagne ou peut être des îles
Printemps relatif arc de triomphe sur mes cils
Tout est calme à droite et dans notre chemin
La colombe est tiède comme un coussin

Le printemps maritime
L'océan tout vert au mois de Mai
L'océan est toujours notre jardin intime
Et les vagues poussent comme des fougeraies

Je veux cette vague de l'horizon
Seul laurier pour mon front

Au fond de mon miroir l'univers se défait
On ne peut rien faire contre le soir qui naît

Behind my eyes
The drowned poet will always sing   [M.P.]

RELATIVITY OF SPRING

You can't do anything about May evenings
Sometimes night comes loose in your hands
And I know your eyes are the end of night

At eight in the morning all the leaves are born
We'll have fruit in place of all those stars

When you go away you lock up the landscape
And no one has tended the sheep by the shore

Spring is relative like a rainbow
It could just as well be a parasol
A parasol over a sigh at noon

Rain puts out the sun

Transalpine parasol or maybe insular
Relative spring triumphal arch above an eyelash
To the right everything's calm and in our path
Like a cushion the dove is lukewarm

Maritime spring
The ocean of May completely green
The ocean remains our private garden
And the waves push up like ferns

I want that wave on the horizon
The only laurel for my brow

In the depths of my mirror the universe comes loose
You can't do anything about evening being born   [M.P.]

CLEF DES SAISONS

Je possède la clef de l'automne
De ma poitrine naissent les feuilles jaunes
Et un soir je dois pleurer tous les ruisseaux

A quoi bon suivre l'oiseau du tout d'un coup
Le jour meurt dans tes joues

Ne pense à rien
Entre les feuilles il y a la nuit qui vient
Il y a une heure qui s'enfuit
Et l'horloge est agreste
Il y a la pluie à gauche et l'aéroplane à l'est

Il y a une musique de harpe qui a frisé tes cheveux
Et au fond du ciel un arbre en feu
Pour dormir la terre s'épanche
Cachée à nos regards sous quelques branches

La pensée moins végétale de la journée
Dans mon doigt s'est posée
Pour attendre ensemble l'aube acide
Toutes les chansons tombèrent de la mésange en vol

Séduisons l'oiseau qui se vide
Et qui meuble des chants les ardoises et le sol

HONNI SOIT QUI MAL Y DANSE . . .

Regardez Madame la lune décroît
Et les fruits se gonflent tous à la fois

Farine d'aveugle et rayons de lune
Le magasin vend son bouquet d'oeuf
Les nuits obéissantes à l'appel des brunes
Quand les planètes tournent dans les yeux du boeuf

KEY TO THE SEASONS

I own the key to autumn
Yellow leaves spring from my breast
And some evening I'll weep all the streams

Why chase the bird of suddenness
When day is dying on your cheeks

Don't think about anything
There's night arriving between the leaves
There's an hour escaping
And the rustic clock
And rain to the left an airplane to the east

There's the harp's music curling your hair
And a tree on fire behind the sky
Hidden from our sight beneath a few branches
The earth spreads out in order to sleep

Daytime's less vegetal thought
Perches on my finger
To wait for the acid dawn
From the chickadee in flight come all the songs

Let's seduce that bird dropping tunes
All over the ground and on every roof   [M.P.]

HONNI SOIT QUI MAL Y DANSE . . .

Look Madame how the moon wanes
And all at once each fruit inflates

Blindman's wheat and moon rays
The store sells its egg bouquet
Nights obey the call of the fog
As the planets turn in a cow's eye

Madame votre oeil en bouteille de mer
Laisse échapper les parfums de mes vers

Les voyageurs venaient sur un fil de fer
Ils venaient en équilibre tels que viennent les mots
Les mots à mi-hauteur parcourent l'univers
Et souvent sont mangés par les oiseaux

Il ne me reste rien, dansez la capucine
Et buvons le couchant comme une grenadine

YA VAS HATCHOU

J'ai été partout et nulle part comme un air de musique

J'ai vu l'amour et le cheval antique
Les vagues de la mer mourant de peste
Le train la vie le pleur qui résoud son théorème

Et niché sur un nuage voyageant vers l'Est
Un oiseau qui chantait oublié de lui-même

Au fond je t'aime
Tu es plus pâle que l'heure et tu fais la légende
Tes paupières sont la seule chose qui s'envole
Et tu es bien plus belle que le retour du pôle

Pendant la nuit
Ton cœur luit

Toi seule vis
Dehors c'est la fin du monde et du violoncelle
Une larme tremble au bord du ciel

La terre s'éloigne et se dégonfle
Tels que tes yeux et ta figure

La chambre s'est vidée par la serrure.

Madame your eye in a bottle at sea
Allows the scent of my verses to escape

The travellers arrived on a steel wire
Perfectly balanced the way words arrive
Words cross the universe at half-mast
And often get eaten by birds

I've nothing left, so dance the capucine
And let's drink the setting sun like a grenadine   [M.P.]

YA VAS HATCHOU

I've been everywhere and nowhere like a tune

I've seen love and the ancient horse
Ocean waves dying of the plague
A train a life a tear solving its theorem

And nesting on a cloud headed toward the East
A bird which sang heedless of itself

Basically I love you
You are paler than an hour and the source of myth
Your eyelids alone take flight
And you're more beautiful by far
          than a return trip from the Arctic

Throughout the night
Your heart gives off light

Only you live
Outside it's the end of the world and of the cello
A tear trembles at the sky's edge

The earth grows distant and deflates
Just like your face and eyes

The room has emptied through the keyhole   [M.P.]

POEME

Colonise la douleur avec ta voix
Enfant de mer sans soucis alterne
Il dort à l'ombre de ma flûte et de ses doigts

Regarde bien mon cœur est une lanterne
Et mes prières montent comme l'arbre en escalier interne

Je te dis que tu es belle
Comme une chambre d'hôtel

Tu cherches l'échelle de corde et le violon civil
Ici sous l'églantine
Et la couronne d'épines
Dis-moi toujours que tu adores mes cils

Si j'étais ruisseau ou bien touriste
Vous m'aimeriez tous comme on aime les artistes
Mais je déteste l'hiver et les draps de l'œil
Et ta petite étoile qui tourne à merveille

J'aime la patience et l'hirondelle
Le lit à voile pour le voyage sans rêve
Quand les vagues rongent la nuit précise
Et la tête monte et le ballon crève
Sous le papier de lune que s'éloigne et glisse
Cherchant les mots qui pendent au ciel

POEM

Colonize sadness with your voice
Child of the sea having no other care
He sleeps in the shade of my flute and his fingers

Watch closely my heart is a beacon
And my prayers climb an inner stair like a tree

I tell you you're beautiful
Like a room in some hotel

Here beneath the eglantine
And the crown of thorns
You look for the rope ladder and the polite violin
Tell me forever you adore my second chin

If I were a stream or a tourist
You'd all love me the way you love artists
But I hate winter and the eye's lids
And your little star wondrous as it turns

I like patience and the swallow
The bed with sails for the dreamless voyage
As waves consume the precise night
And the head rises and the balloon bursts
Under the paper moon which slides away
Looking for the words hung from the sky   [M.P.]

Tout A Coup

Suddenly

1925

2

Sur le miroir une araignée qui rame comme une barque régulière
Vers les chansons du marécage
Elle chatouille les souvenirs à la surface et les gestes derrière
Au milieu du silence la mer naufrage

A l'heure des hirondelles
Dieu que les femmes sont belles
Ta femme a les cheveux blonds neufs
Ses yeux sont des jaunes d'œufs
Les yeux des brunes
Sont des jaunes de lune

Parmi les eaux sans musique
Les regards satellites
Se promènent sous les arbres de l'orbite

3

Je m'éloigne en silence comme un ruban de soie
Promeneur de ruisseaux
Tous les jours je me noie
Au milieu des plantations de prières
Les cathédrales de mes tendresses chantent la nuit sous l'eau
Et ces chants font les îles de la mer

Je suis le promeneur
Le promeneur qui ressemble aux quatre saisons
Le bel oiseau navigateur
Etait comme une horloge entourée de coton
Avant de s'envoler m'a dit ton nom

L'horizon colonial est tout couvert de draperies
Allons dormir sous l'arbre pareil à la pluie

2

On the mirror a spider rowing like a regular boat
Toward songs of the marsh
She tickles memories to the surface and leaves deeds behind
In the midst of silence the sea shipwrecks

At the hour of swallows
God how the women are lovely
Yours has new blond hair
Her eyes are egg yokes
The eyes of brunettes
Are moon yellow

Amid the waters without music
Satellite glances
Are walking under trees of the orbit   [G.Y.]

3

I withdraw in silence like a silk ribbon
Stream walker
Every day I am drowned
In the greenhouse of prayers
The cathedrals of my tenderness sing the night under water
And these songs make islands in the sea

I am the one who walks
And I am like the four seasons
The beautiful seafaring bird
Was like a clock wrapped in cotton
Before flying off it told me your name

The colonial horizon is smothered with flags
Let's go to sleep under the tree
Just like the rain   [G.Y.]

1 0

Elle disait des phrases rondes commes des bagues
Elle répétait le discours des vagues
Elle parlait parlait

Sors mon petit violoncelle
Sors ma lune bien-aimée
Sors te promener
Comme un aveugle ou comme une épée

Monte jusqu'au dernier étage
Alors elle pourra dire à mes amis
Connais-tu le pays
Je connais le pays

Elle nous dira tout bas comme une abeille sincère
Les racontars astronomiques de l'univers
Avec un bon goût de coquillage
Petit gramophone des plages
Qui garde jaloux les secrets de la mer

Elle pourra dire à mes amis
Messieurs la lune se décolle
J'ai compté toutes les monnaies de l'infini
La rose qui manque au pôle
                                        La voici

3 0

Madame il y a trop d'oiseaux
Dans votre piano
Qui attire l'automne sur une forêt
Epaise des nerfs palpitants et des libellules

Les arbres en arpèges insoupçonnés
Perdent parfois l'orientation du globe

Madame je supporte tout. Sans chloroforme
Je descends au fond de l'aube

1 0

She was saying sentences round as rings
She was repeating the discourse of the waves
She was talking talking

Come forth my little cello
Come my beloved moon
Come take a walk
Like a blind man or a sword

Climb to the highest floor
Then she'll be able to say to my friends
Do you know the country
I know the country

She'll tell us everything in the hushed voice of a sincere bee
Astronomic gossips of the universe
With a fine taste for shellfish
Tiny record player of the beaches
Jealously guarding the sea's secrets

She'll be able to tell my friends
Gentlemen the moon is unglued
I have counted all the coins of infinity
The rose missing at the pole
                              Here it is   [G.Y.]

3 0

Lady there are too many birds
In your piano
Dragging autumn over a thick
Forest of palpitating nerves and dragonflies

Sometimes the trees
In unsuspected arpeggios
Lose their global orientation

Lady I can bear anything. Without chloroform
I go down to the depths of dawn

Le rossignol roi de septembre m'informe
Que la nuit se laisse tomber entre la pluie
Trompant la vigilance de vos regards
Et qu'une voix chante loin de la vie
Pour soutenir l'espace décloué
L'espace si lourd d'étoiles qu'il va tomber

Madame dix heures sent le tabac d'artiste
Vous aimez le nadir au corps d'oiseau
Vous êtes un phénomène léger
Je m'en vais tout seul au couchant des touristes
C'est bien plus beau

3 2

Sur le chemin de gauche la saison fuit
Les pigeons dévalent le silence en petits morceaux
Pourquoi ton cœur fait trop de bruit
C'est l'heure où les poissons attentifs comme des fruits de patience
Ecoutent descendre le temps au fond de l'eau

Notre vie est parfumée par la distance
Et je suis parallèle parmi les feuilles intégrales
Sur cette campagne au gosier de colombe
Je mange la même nourriture de doléances

Mes colombes s'évanouissent d'émotion spéciale
Le matin calculé de l'harmonium sincère

Lève les regards vers les plus planètes
Le créateur des rayons visuels et de l'époque tertiaire
Qui a la langue en fer rouge comme les prophètes

The nightingale King of September informs me
That night is dropping into the rain
Deceiving the vigilance of your eyes
And that far from life a voice sings
To pillar unhinged space
Space so heavy with stars it must fall

Lady ten o'clock smells of artists' tobacco
You love slumming with your bird's body
You are a weightless phenomenon
I'm going alone to the sunset of tourists
It's a lot better looking   [G.Y.]

3 2

The season flees on the left road
Pigeons lower silence in tiny morsels
That's why your heart makes too much noise
It is the hour when fish
Attentive as the fruits of patience
Listen as time drops to the bottom of the water

Our life is perfumed by distance
And I lie parallel amid unbroken leaves
Over this countryside in the dove's throat
I eat the same food of grievances

My doves faint from the intense emotion
The calculated morning of the sincere harmonium

Lift your sights toward the further planets
The creator of visual rays and the tertiary epoch
Whose tongue is made of red iron like the prophets

[G.Y.]

Manifestes

Manifestos

1925

MANIFESTO PERHAPS

No true road, and a poetry skeptical of itself.

And then? The search goes on.

In scattered tremblings my nerves without guitar, without qualms, the thing thus conceived far from the poem, to steal snow from the pole and the pipe from the sailor.

A few days later I figured out the pole was a pearl for my tie.

And the Explorers?

They became poets and sang upright on the spilled waves.

And the Poets?

They became explorers and looked for crystal in the throats of nightingales.

That is why Poet equals Globe-trotter without active profession, and Globe-trotter equals Poet without passive profession.

Especially necessary to sing or simply speak without mandatory double meaning, but a few disciplined waves.

No fictive heights, only the true which is organic. Leave the sky to astronomers, cells to cytologists.

The poet is not always a telescope able to change into its opposite, and if a star slides up to the eye through the hollow of the tube, it's not like an elevator, but a magic lens.

No machine or modernity for its own sake. No gulf-stream or cocktail, because gulf-stream and cocktail have become more machine than a locomotive or a deep sea diver, and more modern than New York and catalogues.

Milan . . . naive city, exhausted virgin of the Alps, virgin still.

AND THE GREAT DANGER TO THE POEM
IS THE POETIC

So I say let's look elsewhere, far from machine and dawn, as far from New York as from Byzantium.

Don't add poetry to what has it already without you. Honey poured on honey, it's sickening.

Let factory smoke and the handkerchiefs of farewell dry in the sun.

Put your shoes in the moonlight and we'll talk of it later, and especially, don't forget that Vesuvius, inspite of futurism, is all full of Gounod.

And the unexpected?

Doubtless it could be a thing presenting itself with the impartiality of an unwilled gesture born of chance, but it is too close to instinct and even more animal than human.

Chance is fine when you're dealt five aces or at least four queens. Otherwise, forget it.

No poem drawn from lots. No one shoots craps on the poet's table.

And if the best poem is made in the throat, it is because the throat is dead center between heart and head.

Make poetry, but don't drape it around things. Invent it.

The poet must no longer be an instrument of nature, but he will make nature his instrument. That's the whole difference with the old schools.

And now a new fact is brought to you, completely simple in its essence, independent of any other external phenomena: a human creation, very pure and polished by the brain with an oyster's patience.

Is it a poem, or something else?

It hardly matters.

It hardly matters that the creature be boy or girl, or that it be lawyer, engineer, or biologist, provided that it be.

It lives and it disturbs, even crouched calmly in its depth.

It is not perhaps the ordinary poem, but nevertheless it is.

Thus: first effect of the poem, transfiguration of our daily Christ, innocent upheaval, eyes wide open to the flowing edge of words, brain descends to the chest and heart rises to head, all the while remaining heart and head with their essential faculties: at last, total revolution. Earth turns backwards, sun rises in the West.

Where are you?

Where am I?

The cardinal points are lost in the shuffle like the four aces in a deck of cards.

Later, you love or you reject, but illusion sat in comfortable chairs, boredom moved at a good clip, and the heart spilled its vial of unconscious odors.

(Love or rejection have no importance for the true poet, for he knows that the world moves from right to left and men from left to right. It's the law of equilibrium.)

And then, it is my hand that has guided you, that has shown you willed landscapes and that has caused a brook to be born from an almond tree without giving it a lance prick in the ribs.

And when the camels of your imagination tried to scatter, I stopped them cold, faster than a thief in the desert.

No idle promenades!

The stock market or life.

There, it's clear, it's clean. No private interpretation.

The market doesn't mean the heart, nor life the eyes.

The market is the market and life is life.

Each line of the poem is the point of an angle that is closing, not the meeting of an angle opening to every wind.

The poem, such as it is presented here, is not realistic, but human.

It is not realistic, but it becomes reality.

Cosmic reality with the right atmosphere and clearly it contains earth and water, just as earth and water embrace all disciplines that honor each other.

You must not look through these poems for a memory of things seen, nor the possibility of seeing other things.

A poem is a poem, just as an orange is an orange, and not an apple.

You will not find things that already existed nor come into direct contact with objects of the external world.

The poet will no longer imitate nature, for he doesn't allow himself the right to plagiarize God.

You will find what you have never seen before: the poem. A creation of man.

And of all human forces, that which interests us the most, is the creative force. [G.Y.]

Beaulieu, 1918. Standing: (from left) Juan Gris, Huidobro, Jacques Lipchitz. Seated: (from left) Josette Gris, Manuela Portales Bello de Huidobro, Berthe Lipchitz. The children are the Huidobros'.

Paris, September of 1923 or 1924. Standing: (from left) Gerardo Diego, unknown man, Paul Dermée, unknown man, Céline Arnauld. Seated: (from right) Manuela Portales Bello de Huidobro, Huidobro, Madame Léger, Daniel Henri Kahnweiler, Fernand Léger, Josette Gris, unknown man, Juan Gris, Madame Kahnweiler.

Huidobro (left) with Hans Arp, Arcachon, France, 1931, during their collaboration on *Tres Inmensas Novelas.*

Vicente Huidobro,
Arcachon, France, 1931.
Photograph by Arp.

Huidobro's apartment at 41 Rue Victor Masse, Paris, 1923. On the mantel, two sculptures by Lipchitz and African art objects. Three of Huidobro's "painted-poems" are in view: "Tour Eiffel" and "Marine" are above the desk and "Un Astre A Perdu Son Chemin" is in front of the fireplace.

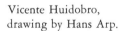

Vicente Huidobro,
drawing by Hans Arp.

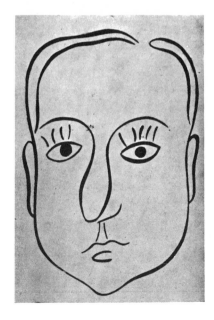

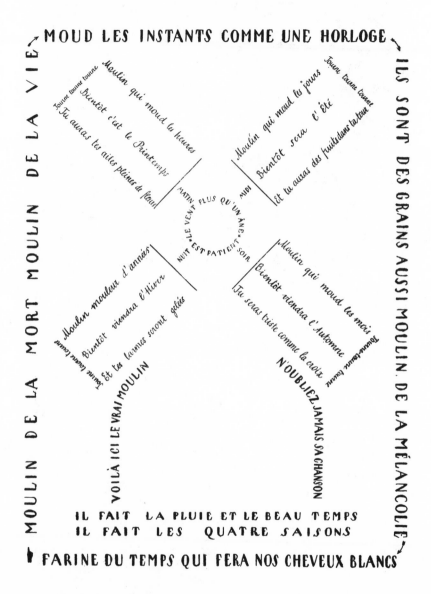

MOUD LES INSTANTS COMME UNE HORLOGE

ILS SONT DES GRAINS AUSSI MOULIN DE LA MÉLANCOLIE

MOULIN DE LA MORT MOULIN DE LA VIE

Moulin qui moud les heures
Tourne tourne tourne
Bientôt c'est le Printemps
Tu auras les ailes pleines de fleurs

Moulin qui moud les jours
Tourne tourne tourne
Bientôt sera l'été
Et tu auras des fruits dans ta tour

MATIN PLUS QU'UN ÂNE MIDI
NUIT LE VENT EST PATIENT SOIR

Moulin moudeur d'années
Bientôt viendra l'Hiver
Tourne tourne tourne
Et tes larmes seront gelées

Moulin qui moud les mois
Bientôt viendra l'Automne
Tourne tourne tourne
Tu seras triste comme la croix

VOILÀ ICI LE VRAI MOULIN

N'OUBLIEZ JAMAIS SA CHANSON

IL FAIT LA PLUIE ET LE BEAU TEMPS
IL FAIT LES QUATRE SAISONS

FARINE DU TEMPS QUI FERA NOS CHEVEUX BLANCS

"Moulin." From Huidobro's *Salle 14* exhibit of "painted-poems," Paris, 1922.

Altazor

or
The Parachute Voyage

Poem in VII Cantos
1919–1931

PREFACE

I was born at thirty-three, the day Christ died; I was born in the Equinox, beneath the hydrangeas and the heat's aeroplanes.

I had a vision as deep as a young pigeon's, like a tunnel and a sentimental automobile. I cast acrobatic sighs.

My father was blind and his hands were more wonderful than the night.

I love the night, hat of each day.

Night, night of the day, from day to following day.

My mother spoke like the dawn, like dirigibles about to drop. She had flag colored hair and eyes full of distant ships.

One afternoon, I got my parachute and said: "With a star and two swallows." Here's death drawing near like earth to a falling planet.

My mother wove deserted tears on the first rainbows.

And now my parachute falls from dream to dream through spaces of death.

The first day I met a strange bird who told me: "If I were a dromedary I wouldn't be thirsty. What time is it?" He drank the dewdrops from my hair, threw me three and a half glances and went off saying: "Adiós" with his magnificent scarf.

That day, around two, I passed a beautiful aeroplane covered with shells and fish scales. It was looking for a place in the sky to hide from the rain.

Far away, all the anchored boats, in the dawn's shade. Suddenly, one by one, they began to break loose, dragging strips of actual dawn like flags.

And as the last ones left, the dawn disappeared behind some great stormy waves.

Then I heard the Creator speak, nameless, just a simple hole in space, as beautiful as a navel:

"I made a great noise and this noise made the ocean and the ocean's waves.

"This noise will be tied to the sea's waves forever and the sea's waves will forever be tied to it, like stamps to a postcard.

"After that I spun a long cord of light beams to sew the days to, one by one—the days of legitimate or reconstituted, yet unquestionable, origin.

"After that I traced the geography of the earth and the lines of the hand.

"After that I drank a little cognac (for the hydrography).

84

"After that I created the mouth and the mouth's lips, to secure ambiguous smiles, and the mouth's teeth, to guard against the curses that come to our mouths.

"I created the tongue which men turned into something else, teaching it how to speak . . . to her, her, the beautiful swimmer, transformed forever from her aquatic and completely caressing being."

My parachute began to dive in a whirl. Such is the great pull of death and the open grave.

You can be sure, the grave has more power than lovers' eyes. The open grave with all its magnets. And I say this to you, you, who when you smile make one think of the beginning of the world.

My parachute tangled on a faded star which was still turning conscientiously, as if unaware of the waste of its efforts.

And taking advantage of this well-earned rest, I began filling the drawers of my desk with profound thoughts:

"Real poems are fires. Poetry is spreading everywhere, lighting its quests with a shuddering of pleasure or pain.

"One should write in a language other than one's mother tongue.

"The four cardinal points are three: South and North.

"A poem is something that will be.

"A poem is something that never is, but should be.

"A poem is something that never has been, that never will be.

"Flee from the outer sublime if you don't want to die crushed by the wind.

"If I didn't act crazy at least once a year, I would go crazy."

I grab my parachute and from the edge of my spinning star I jump into the atmosphere of the final sigh.

Endlessly I fall above the rocks of dreams, I fall amid the clouds of death.

I meet the Virgin seated on a rose, and she says to me:

"Look at my hands: they are as lucid as light bulbs. Do you see the filaments from which my pure light's blood flows?

"Look at my halo. It has some cracks in it which prove my great age.

"I am the Virgin, the Virgin without a trace of human stain, the only true one, the head of the other eleven thousand who were really too remodeled.

"I speak a language that fills hearts according to the law of the communicating clouds.

"I always say good-bye, and stay.

"Love me, my son, since I love your poetry and will teach you aerial prowess.

"I need tenderness so much, kiss my hair, which I washed this morning in the dawn's mists and now I want to sleep on a bed of intermittent drizzle.

"My glances are a wire on the horizon for sparrows to rest on.

"Love me."

I knelt down in circling space and the Virgin rose and seated herself on my parachute.

I slept and it was then that I recited my most beautiful poems.

The flames of my poetry dried the hair of the Virgin who thanked me and went off on her delicate rose.

And here I am, alone, like the nameless shipwreck's little orphan.

Ah, how beautiful . . . how beautiful.

I see mountains, rivers, forests, oceans, ships, flowers and seashells.

I see the night and the day and the point where they join.

Ah, ah, I am Altazor, the great poet, without a horse that eats birdseed or warms its throat with moonlight, but with my little parachute like a parasol above the planets.

From each drop of sweat that falls from my forehead new planets are born which I leave to you to baptize with bottles of wine.

I see it all, my mind is forged in the tongues of a prophet.

The mountain is the sigh of God, rising like a swollen thermometer till it touches the feet of the loved one.

The one who's seen it all, the one who knows all the secrets without being Walt Whitman, since I've never had a beard white as beautiful nurses and frozen streams.

The one who during the night listens to the hammers of the counterfeiters, who are only astronomers working.

The one who drinks the warm glass of wisdom after the flood of doves and knows the road of pain, the seething wake the ships leave behind.

The one who knows the storehouses of memories and beautiful forgotten seasons.

Him, the shepherd of aeroplanes, the guide to lost nights and west winds trained by the lonely poles.

His moan is like a blinking net of invisible aerolites.

The sun rises in your heart and lowers its eyelids to bring the night of agricultural sleep.

Wash your hands in the glance of God, and do your hair like light and the harvest of those few kernels of satisfied rain.

The screams go off like a flock of sheep over the hills when the stars go to sleep after a night of continuous work.

The beautiful hunter in front of the heartless birds' heavenly fountain.

Be as sad as gazelles before the infinite and meteors, like deserts without mirages.

Until the arrival of a mouth swollen with kisses for the harvest of exile.

Be sad, since she waits for you in a part of this year which is passing.

Perhaps she's at the end of your next song and will be as beautiful as a waterfall in motion and as delicate as the equatorial line.

Be sad, sadder than the rose, beautiful cage of our glances and of innocent bees.

Life is a parachute voyage and not what you'd like to think.

Let's go, let's start falling, let's fall from zenith to nadir, let's stain the air with blood so those that come tomorrow will be poisoned when they breathe it.

Inside yourself, outside yourself, you will fall from zenith to nadir because that's your fate, your horrible fate. And the further you fall, the higher your rebound will be, the greater your duration in the stone's memory.

We leapt from the belly of our mother or from the edge of a star and now we're falling.

Ah, my parachute, the air's only perfumed rose, the rose of death, thrust among the stars of death.

Have you heard it? That's the sinister sound of locked breasts.

Open the door of your soul and come out and breathe. With a sigh you can open the door the hurricane closed.

Man, here's your parachute, marvelous as vertigo.

Poet, here's your parachute, marvelous as the pull of the void.

Magician, here's your parachute, which just a word from you can change into a paralifter marvelous as the lightning that would like to blind God.

What are you waiting for?

Here too is the secret of Darkness which forgot to smile.

And the parachute sits tied to the gate like the horse of endless flight.

[D.M.G.]

from **CANTO I**

Altazor ¿por qué perdiste tu primera serenidad?
¿Qué ángel malo se paró en la puerta de tu sonrisa
Con la espada en la mano?
¿Quién sembró la angustia en las llanuras de tus ojos como el adorno
    de un dios?
¿Por qué un día de repente sentiste el terror de ser?
Y esa voz que te gritó vives y no te ves vivir
¿Quién hizo converger tus pensamientos al cruce de todos los vientos
    del dolor?
Se rompió el diamante de tus sueños en un mar de estupor
Estás perdido Altazor
Solo en medio del universo
Solo como una nota que florece en las alturas del vacío
No hay bien no hay mal ni verdad ni orden ni belleza

¿En dónde estás Altazor?

La nebulosa de la angustia pasa como un río
Y me arrastra según la ley de las atracciones
La nebulosa en olores solidificada huye su propia soledad
Siento un telescopio que me apunta como un revólver
La cola de un cometa me azota el rostro y pasa relleno de eternidad
Buscando infatigable un lago quieto en donde refrescar su tarea inelu-
    dible

Altazor morirás Se secará tu voz y serás invisible
La Tierra seguirá girando sobre su órbita precisa
Temerosa de un traspié como el equilibrista sobre el alambre que ata
    las miradas del pavor
En vano buscas ojo enloquecido
No hay puerta de salida y el viento desplaza los planetas
Piensas que no importa caer eternamente si se logra escapar
¿No ves que vas cayendo ya?
Limpia tu cabeza de prejuicio y moral
Y si queriendo alzarte nada has alcanzado
Déjate caer sin parar tu caída sin miedo al fondo de la sombra
Sin miedo al enigma de ti mismo
Acaso encuentres una luz sin noche
Perdida en las grietas de los precipicios

from CANTO I

Altazor how did you lose your first serenity?
What evil angel landed at your gate your smile
With sword in hand?
Who planted anguish in the plains inside your eyes a god's adornment?
Why one day—in a flash—did you feel the terror of existence?
And that voice that hollered at you you're alive & you can't see that
    you're alive
Who made your thoughts meet at these crossroads for all grieving
    winds?
The diamond in your dreams cracked open in a mindless sea
You are lost Altazor
You're alone at the universe's center
Alone like a dot that blossoms high over the void
There's no good no evil no truth no order no beauty

Where are you at Altazor?

The nebula—anguish—passes by like a river
And drags me down by the law of affinities
The nebula changed into solidified smells eludes its own loneliness
I can feel how a telescope points at my head like a gun
A comet's tail beats on my face & passes by stuffed with eternity
Tireless seeking a lake with no sounds a break from inevitable angst

Altazor you will die Your voice will dry up & you will become invisible
The Earth will continue to turn in its precise orbit
In terror of tumbling like an acrobat out on a wire its rope ends tied
    to the wide eyes of fear
You will hunt in vain for some maddened eye
But there's no way out & the wind displaces the planets
You think it doesn't matter falling forever if you somehow escape in
    the end
Don't you see that you're falling already?
It's time you were rid of morals & prejudice
If you try to rise & you stumble towards nothing
Let yourself fall without stopping without fear to the deep end of dark-
    ness
To the baffled cry of your Self
Maybe you'll find a sun that can't set
Lost in the fissures of cliffs

Cae
    Cae eternamente
Cae al fondo del infinito
Cae al fondo del tiempo
Cae al fondo de ti mismo
Cae lo más bajo que se pueda caer
Cae sin vértigo
A través de todos los espacios y todas las edades
A través de todas las almas de todos los anhelos y todos los naufragios
Cae y quema al pasar los astros y los mares
Quema los ojos que te miran y los corazones que te aguardan
Quema el viento con tu voz
El viento que se enreda en tu voz
Y la noche que tiene frío en su gruta de huesos

Cae en infancia
Cae en vejez
Cae en lágrimas
Cae en risas
Cae en música sobre el universo
Cae de tu cabeza a tus pies
Cae de tus pies a tu cabeza
Cae del mar a la fuente
Cae al último abismo de silencio
Como el barco que se hunde apagando sus luces

Todo se acabó
El mar antropófago golpea la puerta de las rocas despiadadas
Los perros ladran a las horas que se mueren
Y el cielo escucha el paso de las estrellas que se alejan
Estás solo
Y vas a la muerte derecho como un iceberg que se desprende del polo
Cae la noche buscando su corazón en el océano
La mirada se agranda como los torrentes
Y en tanto que las olas se dan vuelta
La luna niño de luz se escapa de alta mar
Mira este cielo lleno
Más rico que los arroyos de las minas
Cielo lleno de estrellas que esperan el bautismo

Fall
  Fall forever
Fall to the depths of the infinite
Fall to the depths of time
Fall to the depths of your Self
Fall as low as you can
Fall without dizziness
Into all spaces & ages
Into each soul each longing for land each shipwreck
Fall
  Scald the stars & the seas as you pass
Scald the eyes that watch you the hearts that await you
Scald the wind with your voice
The wind that's trapped in your voice
And the night growing cold in its cave filled with bones

Fall into childhood
Fall into age
Fall into tears
Fall into laughter
Fall into music all over the universe
Fall from your head to your feet
Fall from your feet to your head
Fall from the sea to its source
Fall to the final abyss of silence
Like a sinking ship drowning its lights

Then it's all over
The man-eating sea beats the doors of those merciless cliffs
Dogs bark at the death of our hours
And the sky hears the footsteps of stars trailing off
You're alone
And heading straight into death you're an iceberg split off from the
    Pole
The night falls it looks for your heart in the ocean
Its look grows wild like those torrents
And just when the waves swing around
The moon—child of light—escapes the high sea
Keeps watching this sky
It's a full sky it's rich like the streams in your mines
It's a sky full of stars preparing for baptism

Todas esas estrellas salpicaduras de un astro de piedra lanzado en las
    aguas eternas
No saben lo que quieren ni si hay redes ocultas más allá
Ni qué mano lleva las riendas
Ni qué pecho sopla el viento sobre ellas
Ni saben si no hay mano y no hay pecho
Las montañas de pesca
Tienen la altura de mis deseos
Y yo arrojo fuera de la noche mis últimas angustias
Que los pájaros cantando dispersan por el mundo

Reparad el motor del alba
En tanto me siento al borde de mis ojos
Para asistir a la entrada de las imágenes

Soy yo Altazor
Altazor
Encerrado en la jaula de su destino
En vano me aferro a los barrotes de la evasión posible
Una flor cierra el camino
Y se levanta como la estatua de las llamas
La evasión imposible
Más débil marcho con mis ansias
Que un ejército sin luz en medio de emboscadas

Abrí los ojos en el siglo
En que moría el cristianismo
Retorcido en su cruz agonizante
Ya va a dar el último suspiro
¿Y mañana qué pondremos en el sitio vacío?
Pondremos un alba o un crepúsculo
¿Y hay que poner algo acaso?
La corona de espinas
Chorreando sus últimas estrellas se marchita
Morirá el cristianismo que no ha resuelto ningún problema
Que sólo ha enseñado plegarias muertas
Muere después de dos mil años de existencia
Un cañoneo enorme pone punto final a la era cristiana
El Cristo quiere morir acompañado de millones de almas
Hundirse con sus templos
Y atravesar la muerte con un cortejo inmenso

All those stars like the splash of a sphere like a rock in primordial
waters
They don't know what they want if the secret nets are still there
Or what hand holds the reins
Or whose breast breathes the wind that blows over them
Or if there's any hand or any breast
The mountains are fisheries
Hills as high as my longings
And I fling my last anguish out past the night
That the songbirds spread through the world

Tune up the dawn's motor
While I sit at the edge of my eyes
And click off the entry of images

This is me Altazor
Altazor
Locked up in his fate like a cage
In vain I grasp the rungs to try a possible escape
A flower blocks the way
And looms up like a statue made of fire
Escape impossible
Strung out I move about more weakly
Than an army without light in the midst of ambushes

I opened my eyes up in the century
That Christianity died out
Contorted on its agonizing cross
About to cough up its last breath
What will we put there tomorrow in that empty space?
We'll put in a dawn or a twilight
And do we really have to put in something?
The crown of thorns
Dribbles its final stars & withers
Christianity will die & leave no problem solved
Only a handful of dead prayers its teachings
Will die after 2000 years of existence
A huge bombardment puts a stopper on the Christian era
Christ wants to die with a cast of millions
To come crashing down with all his temples
To cross over into death with an immense cortege

Mil aeroplanos saludan la nueva era
Ellos son los oráculos y las banderas

Hace seis meses solamente
Dejé la ecuatorial recién cortada
En la tumba guerrera del esclavo paciente
Corona de piedad sobre la estupidez humana
Soy yo que estoy hablando en este año de 1919
Es el invierno
Ya la Europa enterró todos sus muertos
Y un millar de lágrimas hacen una sola cruz de nieve
Mirad esas estepas que sacuden las manos
Millones de obreros han comprendido al fin
Y levantan al cielo sus banderas de aurora
Venid venid os esperamos porque sois la esperanza
La única esperanza
La última esperanza

Soy yo Altazor el doble de mí mismo
El que se mira obrar y se ríe del otro frente a frente
El que cayó de las alturas de su estrella
Y viajó veinticinco años
Colgado al paracaídas de sus propios prejuicios
Soy yo Altazor el del ansia infinita
Del hambre eterno y descorazonado
Carne labrada por arados de angustia
¿Cómo podré dormir mientras haya adentro tierras desconocidas?
Problemas
Misterios que se cuelgan a mi pecho
Estoy solo
La distancia que va de cuerpo a cuerpo
Es tan grande como la que hay de alma a alma
Solo
    Solo
       Solo
Estoy solo parado en la punta del año que agoniza
El universo se rompe en olas a mis pies
Los planetas giran en torno a mi cabeza
Y me despeinan al pasar con el viento que desplazan
Sin dar una respuesta que llene los abismos

A thousand airplanes are saluting the new era
They are its oracles & flags

And just six months ago
I left the equatorial line freshly cut
In the martial tomb of some long-suffering slave
A pious crown for human ignorance
This is me talking now in 1919
When it's winter
And Europe has buried all its dead
And a million tears become a single cross of snow
Look at those steppes how they're shaking their fists
Millions of workers have seen the light at last
And raise their flags to heaven like the dawn
Come on workers we've been waiting for you you're our hope
The only hope
The last hope

I'm Altazor the double of myself
Who sees himself at work laughs at the other to his face
Who fell down from his high spot from his star
And voyaged twenty-five years
Hanging from his parachute his preconceptions
I'm Altazor the man of endless longings
Eternal & depressive hunger
Meat worked by plows of anguish
How can I sleep with so many unknown lands inside?
Such problems
Mysteries hanging down my chest
I'm alone
The distances between our bodies
Are as great as those between our souls
Alone
    Alone
       Alone
I'm alone I'm stuck at the tail end of this dead year
The universe's waves break at my feet
The planets swirl around my head
And mess my hair up with their passing winds
Without an answer that could fill their chasms
                     [J.R.]

CANTO III

Romper las ligaduras de las venas
Los lazos de la respiración y las cadenas

De los ojos senderos de horizontes
Flor proyectada en cielos uniformes

El alma pavimentada de recuerdos
Como estrellas talladas por el viento

El mar es un tejado de botellas
Que en la memoria del marino sueña

Cielo es aquella larga cabellera intacta
Tejida entre manos de aeronauta

Y el avión trae un lenguaje diferente
Para la boca de los cielos de siempre

Cadenas de miradas nos atan a la tierra
Romped romped tantas cadenas

Vuela el primer hombre a iluminar el día
El espacio se quiebra en una herida

Y devuelve la bala al asesino
Eternamente atado al infinito

Cortad todas las amarras
De río mar o de montaña

De espíritu y recuerdo
De ley agonizante y sueño enfermo

Es el mundo que torna y sigue y gira
En una última pupila

Mañana el campo
Seguirá los galopes del caballo

La flor se comerá a la abeja
Porque el hangar será colmena

El arco iris se hará pájaro
Y volará a su nido cantando

CANTO III

Break the ligatures of the veins
The loops of respiration and the chains

Of eyes paths of horizons
Flower screened on uniform skies

Soul paved with recollections
Like stars carved by the wind

The sea is a roof of bottles
That dreams in the sailor's memory

The sky is that great whole mane
Woven between the hands of the aeronaut

And the airplane carries a new language
To the mouth of the eternal skies

Chains of glances tie us to the earth
Break them break so many chains

The first man flies to light the sky
Space bursts open in a wound

And the bullet returns to the assassin
Eternally tied to the infinite

Cut all the links
Of river sea or mountain

Of spirit and memory
Of agonizing law and fever dreams

It is the world that turns and follows and whirls
In an ultimate pupil

Tomorrow the countryside
Will follow the galloping horses

The flower will suck the bee
Because the hangar will be a hive

The rainbow will become a bird
And fly singing to its nest

Los cuervos se harán planetas
Y tendrán plumas de hierba

Hojas serán las plumas entibiadas
Que caerán de sus gargantas

Las miradas serán ríos
Y los ríos heridas en las piernas del vacío

Conducirá el rebaño a su pastor
Para que duerma el día cansado como avión

Y el árbol se posará sobre la tórtola
Mientras las nubes se hacen roca

Porque todo es como es en cada ojo
Dinastía astrológica y efímera
Cayendo de universo en universo

Manicura de la lengua es el poeta
Mas no el mago que apaga y enciende
Palabras estelares y cerezas de adioses vagabundos
Muy lejos de las manos de la tierra
Y todo lo que dice es por él inventado
Cosas que pasan fuera del mundo cotidiano
Matemos al poeta que nos tiene saturados

Poesía aún y poesía poesía
Poética poesía poesía
Poesía poética de poético poeta
Poesía
Demasiada poesía
Desde el arco iris hasta el culo pianista de la vecina
Basta señora poesía bambina
Y todavía tiene barrotes en los ojos
El juego es juego y no plegaria infatigable
Sonrisa o risa y no lamparillas de pupila
Que ruedan de la aflicción hasta el océano
Sonrisa y habladurías de estrella tejedora
Sonrisa del cerebro que evoca estrellas muertas
En la mesa mediúmnica de sus irradiaciones

Basta señora arpa de las bellas imágenes
De los furtivos comos iluminados

The crows will become planets
And sprout feathers of grass

Leaves will be tepid feathers
Falling from their throats

Glances will be rivers
And the rivers wounds in the legs of space

The flock will be guided to its pastor
So the day can doze drowsy as an airplane

And the tree will rest on the turtledove
While the clouds turn to stone

Because everything is as it is in every eye
Ephemeral and astrological dynasty
Falling from universe to universe

The poet is the manicurist of the language
And even more the magician who inflames and quenches
Stellar words and the cherries of vagabond good-byes
Far from the hands of the earth
And he invents all that he says
Things that move outside the ordinary world
Let us kill the poet who gluts us

Poetry still and poetry poetry
Poetical poetry poetry
Poetical poetry by poetical poets
Poetry
Too much poetry
From the rainbow to the asshole pianist of the neighborhood
Enough poetry lady enough bambina
It still has bars over its eyes
The game is a game and not an endless prayer
Smiles or laughter and not the pupil's lamps
That wheel from affliction toward the sea
Smile and gossip of the weaver star
Smile of the brain that evokes dead stars
On the mediumistic table of its radiations

Enough lady harp of beautiful images
Of secret illuminated "likes"

Otra cosa otra cosa buscamos
Sabemos posar un beso como una mirada
Plantar miradas como árboles
Enjaular árboles como pájaros
Regar pájaros como heliotropos
Tocar un heliotropo como una música
Vaciar una música como un saco
Degollar un saco como un pingüino
Cultivar pingüinos como viñedos
Ordeñar un viñedo como una vaca
Desarbolar vacas como veleros
Peinar un velero como un cometa
Desembarcar cometas como turistas
Embrujar turistas como serpientes
Cosechar serpientes como almendras
Desnudar una almendra como un atleta
Leñar atletas como cipreses
Iluminar cipreses como faroles
Anidar faroles como alondras
Exhalar alondras como suspiros
Bordar suspiros como sedas
Derramar sedas como ríos
Tremolar un río como una bandera
Desplumar una bandera como un gallo
Apagar un gallo como un incendio
Bogar en incendios como en mares
Segar mares como trigales
Repicar trigales como campanas
Desangrar campanas como corderos
Dibujar corderos como sonrisas
Embotellar sonrisas como licores
Engastar licores como alhajas
Electrizar alhajas como crepúsculos
Tripular crepúsculos como navíos
Descalzar un navío como un rey
Colgar reyes como auroras
Crucificar auroras como profetas
Etc. etc. etc.
Basta señor violín hundido en una ola ola
Cotidiana ola de religión miseria
De sueño en sueño posesión de pedrerías

Something else something else we are seeking
We know how to dart a kiss like a glance
Plant glances like trees
Cage trees like birds
Water birds like heliotropes
Play a heliotrope like music
Empty music like a sack
Decapitate a sack like a penguin
Cultivate penguins like vineyards
Milk a vineyard like a cow
Unmast cows like schooners
Comb a schooner like a comet
Disembark comets like tourists
Bewitch tourists like snakes
Harvest snakes like almonds
Undress an almond like an athlete
Chop down athletes like cypresses
Light cypresses like lanterns
Nestle lanterns like skylarks
Breathe skylarks like sighs
Embroider sighs like silks
Drain silks like rivers
Hoist a river like a flag
Pluck a flag like a rooster
Quench a rooster like a fire
Row through fires like seas
Reap seas like wheatfields
Chime wheatfields like bells
Bleed bells like lambs
Draw lambs like smiles
Bottle smiles like liquor
Set liquor like jewels
Electrify jewels like twilights
Man twilights like battleships
Unshoe a battleship like a king
Raise kings like dawns
Crucify dawns like prophets
Etc. etc. etc.
Enough sir violin sunk in a wave wave
Everyday wave of misery religion
Of dream on dream possessions of jewels

Después del corazón comiendo rosas
Y de las noches del rubí perfecto
El nuevo atleta salta sobre la pista mágica
Jugando con magnéticas palabras
Caldeadas como la tierra cuando va a salir un volcán
Lanzando sortilegios de sus frases pájaro

Agoniza el último poeta
Tañen las campanas de los continentes
Muere la luna con su noche a cuestas
El sol se saca del bolsillo el día
Abre los ojos el nuevo paisaje solemne
Y pasa desde la tierra a las constelaciones
El entierro de la poesía

Todas las lenguas están muertas
Muertas en manos del vecino trágico
Hay que resucitar las lenguas
Con sonoras risas
Con vagones de carcajadas
Con cortacircuitos en las frases
Y cataclismo en la gramática
Levántate y anda
Estira las piernas anquilosis salta
Fuegos de risa para el lenguaje tiritando de frío
Gimnasia astral para las lenguas entumecidas
Levántate y anda
Vive vive como un balón de fútbol
Estalla en la boca de diamantes motocicleta
En ebriedad de sus luciérnagas
Vértigo sí de su liberación
Una bella locura en la vida de la palabra
Una bella locura en la zona del lenguaje
Aventura forrada de desdenes tangibles
Aventura de la lengua entre dos naufragios
Catástrofe preciosa en los rieles del verso

Y puesto que debemos vivir y no nos suicidamos
Mientras vivamos juguemos
El simple sport de los vocablos
De la pura palabra y nada más
Sin imagen limpia de joyas

After the heart eating roses
And the nights of the perfect ruby
The new athlete leaps on the magic track
Frolicking with magnetic words
Hot as the earth when a volcano rises
Hurling the sorceries of his bird phrases

The ultimate poet agonizes
The bells of the continents chime
The moon dies with the night on its back
The sun pulls the day out of its pocket
The solemn new land opens its eyes
And moves from earth to the stars
The burial of poetry

All the languages are dead
Dead in the hands of the tragic neighbor
We must revive the languages
With raucous laughter
With wagons of giggles
With circuit breakers in the sentences
And cataclysm in the grammar
Get up and walk
Stretch your legs limber the stiff joints
Fires of laughter for the shivering language
Astral gymnastics for the numb tongues
Get up and walk
Live live like a football
Explode in the mouth of motorcycle diamonds
In the drunkenness of its fireflies
The very vertigo of its liberation
A beautiful madness in the life of the word
A beautiful madness in the zone of language
Adventure clothed in tangible disdains
The adventure of language between two wrecked ships
Precious catastrophe on the rails of verse

And since we must live and not kill ourselves
As long as we live let us play
The simple game of words
Of the pure word and nothing more
Without clean images of jewels

(Las palabras tienen demasiada carga)
Un ritual de vocablos sin sombra
Juego de ángel allá en el infinito
Palabra por palabra
Con luz propia de astro que un choque vuelve vivo
Saltan chispas del choque y mientras más violento
Más grande es la explosión
Pasión del juego en el espacio
Sin alas de luna y pretensión
Combate singular entre el pecho y el cielo
Total desprendimiento al fin de voz de carne
Eco de luz que sangra aire sobre el aire

Después nada nada
Rumor aliento de frase sin palabra

from **CANTO IV**

No hay tiempo que perder
Todo esto es triste como el niño que está quedándose huérfano
O como la letra que cae al medio del ojo
O como la muerte del perro de un ciego
O como el río que se estira en su lecho de agonizante
Todo esto es hermoso como mirar el amor de los gorriones
Tres horas después del atentado celeste
O como oír dos pájaros anónimos que cantan a la misma azucena
O como la cabeza de la serpiente donde sueña el opio
O como el rubí nacido de los deseos de una mujer
Y como el mar que no se sabe si ríe o llora
Y como los colores que caen del cerebro de las mariposas
Y como la mina de oro de las abejas
Las abejas satélites del nardo como las gaviotas del barco
Las abejas que llevan la semilla en su interior
Y van más perfumadas que pañuelos de narices
Aunque no son pájaros
Pues no dejan sus iniciales en el cielo
En la lejanía del cielo besada por los ojos
Y al terminar su viaje vomitan el alma de los pétalos

(Words carry too much weight)
A ritual of words without shadow
An angel game there in the infinite
Word by word
With the light of a star that a collision brings to life
Sparks leap from the collision and then more violent
More enormous the explosion
Passion of the game in space
Without moon-wings and pretense
Single combat between chest and sky
Total dissolution at last of the voice from flesh
Echo of light that bleeds air over the air

Then nothing nothing
Spirit whisper of the wordless phrase   [E.W.]

from C A N T O   I V

There's no time to lose
All this so sad like the child who's left an orphan
Like the letter that falls in the middle of an eye
Like the dog's death of a blind man
Like the river stretching out on its deathbed
All this so lovely like watching sparrow love
Three hours after the celestial transgression
Like hearing two anonymous birds singing to the same lily
Like the snake's head where opium dreams
Like the ruby born of a woman's desires
Like the sea that doesn't know if it laughs or cries
Like the colors that fall from the brains of butterflies
Like the gold mine of the bees
Bees satellites to spikenard like sea gulls to a boat
The bees that carry the seed within
And drift off more perfumed than a handkerchief
Though they are not birds
And do not leave their monograms on the sky
On the far-off eye-kissed sky
And at journey's end they vomit the petals' soul

Como las gaviotas vomitan el horizonte
Y las golondrinas el verano

No hay tiempo que perder
Ya viene la golondrina monotémpora
Trae un acento antípoda de lejanías que se acercan
Viene gondoleando la golondrina

Al horitaña de la montazonte
La violondrina y el goloncelo
Descolgada esta mañana de la lunala
Se acerca a todo galope
Ya viene viene la golondrina
Ya viene viene la golonfina
Ya viene la golontrina
Ya viene la goloncima
Viene la golonchina
Viene la golonclima
Ya viene la golonrima
Ya viene la golonrisa
La golonniña
La golongira
La golonlira
La golonbrisa
La golonchilla
Ya viene la golondía
Y la noche encoge sus uñas como el leopardo
Ya viene la golontrina
Que tiene un nido en cada uno de los dos calores
Como yo lo tengo en los cuatro horizontes
Viene la golonrisa
Y las olas se levantan en la punta de los pies
Viene la golonniña
Y siente un vahído la cabeza de la montaña
Viene la golongira
Y el viento se hace parábola de sílfides en orgía
Se llenan de notas los hilos telefónicos
Se duerme el ocaso con la cabeza escondida
Y el árbol con el pulso afiebrado

Pero el cielo prefiere el rodoñol
Su niño querido el rorreñol

As sea gulls vomit the horizon
And hirondelles the summer

There's no time to lose
Here alights the monotempory hirondelle
Bringing an antipodal tone of approaching distance
Herein dwells the hirondelle

At the horitain of the mountizon
The violondelle and the hironcello
Slipping down this morning from a lunawing
It hurries near
Here alights alights the hirondelle
Here alights alights the clearondelle
Here alights the trillondelle
Here alights the hillondelle
Alights the chippondelle
Alights the whiffondelle
Here alights the chirpondelle
Here alights the cheerondelle
The girlondelle
The whirlondelle
The lyrondelle
The chillondelle
The shrillondelle
Here alights the hironday
And the night withdraws its claws like a leopard
Here alights the trillondelle
With a nest in each torrid zone
As I have them on the four horizons
Alights the cheerondelle
And waves rise on tiptoe
Alights the girlondelle
And the mountain's head feels dizzy
Alights the whirlondelle
And the wind's a parabola of orgiastic sylphs
The telephone wires fill with notes
The sunset sleeps with hidden head
And the tree with fevered pulse

But the sky prefers the nighdongale
Its favorite sun the nighrengale

Su flor de alegría el romiñol
Su piel de lágrima el rofañol
Su garganta nocturna el rosolñol
El rolañol
El rosiñol

· · ·

Yo no tengo orgullos de campanario
Ni tengo ningún odio petrificado
Ni grito como un sombrero afectuoso que viene saliendo del desierto
Digo solamente
No hay tiempo que perder
El visir con lenguaje de pájaro
Nos habla largo largo como un sendero
Las caravanas se alejan sobre su voz
Y los barcos hacia horizontes imprecisos
El devuelve el oriente sobre las almas
Que toman un oriente de perla
Y se llenan de fósforos a cada paso
De su boca brota una selva
De su selva brota un astro
Del astro cae una montaña sobre la noche
De la noche cae otra noche
Sobre la noche del vacío
La noche lejos tan lejos que parece una muerta que se llevan
Adiós hay que decir adiós
Adíos hay que decir a Dios
Entonces el huracán destruido por la luz de la lengua
Se deshace en arpegios circulares
Y aparece la luna seguida de algunas gaviotas
Y sobre el camino
Un caballo que se va agrandando a medida que se aleja

Darse prisa darse prisa
Están prontas las semillas
Esperando una orden para florecer
Paciencia ya luego crecerán
Y se irán por los senderos de la savia
Por su escalera personal
Un momento de descanso
Antes del viaje al cielo del árbol

Its flower of joy the nighmingale
Its skin of tears the nighfangale
Its nocturnal throat the nighsolngale
The nighlangale
The nightingale

· · ·

I have no towering pride
Nor any petrified hate
I don't shout like a beloved hat that comes out from the desert
I only say
There's no time to lose
The vizier in bird language
Speaks to us long long as a path
Caravans move off over his voice
And ships toward blurred horizons
He restores the orient to souls
That eat orient of pearl
And stuff themselves with matches at every step
A forest sprouts from his mouth
A star sprouts from his forest
From the star a mountain falls on the night
From the night another night falls
On the night of the void
The far-off night so far off it seems like a dead woman they carry
Good-bye one must say good-bye
Good-bye one must say to God
Then the hurricane wrecked by the tongue's light
Unravels in circular arpeggios
And the moon appears followed by gulls
And on the road
A horse goes off growing larger as it goes

Hurry up hurry up
The seeds are ready
Waiting for the order to flower
Patience now then they will grow
And travel through the paths of sap
Along their private stairway
A minute of rest
Before the tree's trip to the sky

El árbol tiene miedo de alejarse demasiado
Tiene miedo y vuelve los ojos angustiados
La noche lo hace temblar
La noche y su licantropía
La noche que afila sus garras en el viento
Y aguza los oídos de la selva
Tiene miedo digo el árbol tiene miedo
De alejarse de la tierra

No hay tiempo que perder
Los icebergs que flotan en los ojos de los muertos
Conocen su camino
Ciego sería el que llorara
Las tinieblas del féretro sin límites
Las esperanzas abolidas
Los tormentos cambiados en inscripción de cementerio
Aquí yace Carlota ojos marítimos
Se le rompió un satélite
Aquí yace Matías en su corazón dos escualos se batían
Aquí yace Marcelo mar y cielo en el mismo violoncelo
Aquí yace Susana cansada de pelear contra el olvido
Aquí yace Teresa ésa es la tierra que araron sus ojos hoy ocupada por
    su cuerpo
Aquí yace Angélica anclada en el puerto de sus brazos
Aquí yace Rosario río de rosas hasta el infinito
Aquí yace Raimundo raíces del mundo son sus venas
Aquí yace Clarisa clara risa enclaustrada en la luz
Aquí yace Alejandro antro alejado ala adentro
Aquí yace Gabriela rotos los diques sube en las savias hasta el sueño
    esperando la resurrección
Aquí yace Altazor azor fulminado por la altura
Aquí yace Vicente antipoeta y mago

Ciego sería el que llorara
Ciego como el cometa que va con su bastón
Y su neblina de ánimas que lo siguen
Obediente al instinto de sus sentidos
Sin hacer caso de los meteoros que apedrean desde lejos
Y viven en colonias según la temporada
El meteoro insolente cruza por el cielo
El meteplata el metecobre

The tree is afraid of going too far
It's afraid and turns back eyes in anguish
Night makes it tremble
The lycanthropic night
The night that files its claws on the wind
And sharpens the sounds of the forest
It's afraid I say the tree is afraid
Of going too far from the earth

There's no time to lose
The icebergs that float in the eyes of the dead
Know the way
He who weeps will be blind
Darkness of the endless crypt
Abandoned hopes
Torments turned to cemetery script
Here lies Charlotte maritime eyes
Broken by a satellite
Here lies Matthias two sharks battled in his heart
Here lies Marcello heaven and hello in the same violoncello
Here lies Susanna weary of struggling against the void
Here lies Teresa till terra erase her eyes
Here lies Angelica anchored in the bay of her arms
Here lies Rosemary rose married to the infinite
Here lies Raymond moonrays are his veins
Here lies Clarissa clear is her smile encloistered in the light
Here lies Alexander alas under till all is yonder
Here lies Gabriela the dam broken she rises with the sap toward the
    dream awaiting resurrection
Here lies Altazor hawk exploded by the height
Here lies Vicente antipoet and magician

He who weeps will be blind
Blind as the comet that travels with its staff
And its mist of souls that follow it
Instinctively obedient to its wishes
Never minding the meteors that pelt from afar
And live in colonies according to the seasons
The insolent meteor crosses the sky
The metesilver the metecopper

El metepiedras en el infinito
Meteópalos en la mirada
Cuidado aviador con las estrellas
Cuidado con la aurora
Que el aeronauta no sea el auricida
Nunca un cielo tuvo tantos caminos como éste
Ni fue tan peligroso
La estrella errante me trae el saludo de un amigo muerto hace diez años
Darse prisa darse prisa
Los planetas maduran en el planetal
Mis ojos han visto la raíz de los pájaros
El más allá de los nenúfares
Y el ante acá de las mariposas
¿Oyes el ruido que hacen las mandolinas al morir?
Estoy perdido
No hay más que capitular
Ante la guerra sin cuartel
Y la emboscada nocturna de estos astros

La eternidad quiere vencer
Y por lo tanto no hay tiempo que perder
Entonces
        Ah entonces
Más allá del último horizonte
Se verá lo que hay que ver
La ciudad
Debajo de las luces y las ropas colgadas
El jugador aéreo
Desnudo
Frágil
La noche al fondo del océano
Tierna ahogada
La muerte ciega
            Y su esplendor
Y el sonido y el sonido
Espacio la lumbrera
            A estribor
            Adormecido
En cruz
      en luz
La tierra y su cielo

The meteorocks in the infinite
The meteopolis in a gaze
Aviator be careful with the stars
Careful with the dawn
That the aeronaut not become an auricide
The sky has never had as many roads as this
Never has it been so treacherous
An errant star brings me greetings from a friend ten years dead
Hurry up hurry up
Planets ripen in the planetary
My eyes have seen the root of birds
The furthest point of waterlilies
And the nearest of butterflies
Do you hear the sound that mandolins make when dying?
I am lost
There is nothing left but capitulation
To the war without quarter
And the nightly ambush of these stars

Eternity waits to conquer
And for that reason there's no time to lose
Then
     Ah then
Farther than the last horizon
What there is to see will be seen
The city
Beneath the lights and the hanging clothes
The aerial trickster
Naked
Fragile
The night at the bottom of the sea
Tender drowned
Blind death
        And its splendor
And the sound and the sound
Space the light-shaft
          Drowsy
          At the starboard
In height
     In light
Earth and its sky

El cielo y su tierra
Selva noche
Y río día por el universo
El pájaro tralalí canta en las ramas de mi cerebro
Porque encontró la clave del eterfinifrete
Rotundo como el unipacio y el espaverso
Uiu uiui
Tralalí tralalá
Aia ai ai aaia i i

CANTO V

Aquí comienza el campo inexplorado
Redondo a causa de los ojos que lo miran
Y profundo a causa de mi propio corazón
Lleno de zafiros probables
De manos de sonámbulos
De entierros aéreos
Conmovedores como el sueño de los enanos
O el ramo cortado en el infinito
Que trae la gaviota para sus hijos

Hay un espacio despoblado
Que es preciso poblar
De miradas con semillas abiertas
De voces bajadas de la eternidad
De juegos nocturnos y aerolitos de violín
De ruido de rebaños sin permiso
Escapados del cometa que iba a chocar
¿Conoces tú la fuente milagrosa
Que devuelve a la vida los náufragos de antaño?
¿Conoces tú la flor que se llama voz de monja
Que crece hacia abajo y se abre al fondo de la tierra?
¿Has visto al niño que cantaba
Sentado en una lágrima
El niño que cantaba al lado de un suspiro
O de un ladrido de perro inconsolable?
¿Has visto al arco iris sin colores
Terriblemente envejecido

Sky and its earth
Forest night
River day through the universe
The bird tralalee sings in the branches of my brain
For I've found the key to the infiniternity
Round as the unimos and the cosverse
Ooheeoo ooheeoohee
Tralalee tralala
Aheeaah ahee ahee aaaheeah ee ee   [E.W.]

CANTO V

Here begins the unexplored ground
Round because of the eyes that see it
And profound because of my own heart
Full of probable sapphires
Of sleepwalkers' hands
Of aerial burials
Unsettling as the dream of dwarfs
Or the branch carved in immensity
The sea gull brings for its little ones

There is an unpopulated area
That must be peopled
In glances with open seeds
In voices sent from eternity
In nocturnal games and violin aerolites
In the noise of unauthorized herds
Escaped from the comet that crashed
Do you know the miraculous fountain
That restored to life the shipwrecked of yore?
Do you know the flower called nun's voice
That grows downward and opens at the depths of the earth?
Have you seen the child who sang
Set in a tear
The child who sang next to a sigh
Or by the barking of an inconsolable dog?
Have you seen the colorless rainbow
Grown terribly old

Que vuelve del tiempo de los faraones?

El miedo cambia la forma de las flores
Que esperan temblando el juicio final
Una a una las estrellas se arrojan por el balcón
El mar se está durmiendo detrás de un árbol
Con su calma habitual
Porque sabe desde los tiempos bíblicos
Que el regreso es desconocido en la estrella polar

Ningún navegante ha encontrado la rosa de los mares
La rosa que trae el recuerdo de sus abuelos
Del fondo de sí misma
Cansada de soñar
Cansada de vivir en cada pétalo
Viento que estás pensando en la rosa del mar
Yo te espero de pie al final de esta línea
Yo sé dónde se esconde la flor que nace del sexo de las sirenas
En el momento del placer
Cuando debajo del mar empieza a atardecer
Y se oye crujir las olas
Bajo los pies del horizonte
Yo sé yo sé dónde se esconde

El viento tiene la voz de abeja de la joven pálida
La joven pálida como su propia estatua
Que yo amé en un rincón de mi vida
Cuando quería saltar de una esperanza al cielo
Y caí de naufragio en naufragio de horizonte en horizonte
Entonces vi la rosa que se esconde
Y que nadie ha encontrado cara a cara

¿Has visto este pájaro de islas lejanas
Arrojado por la marea a los pies de mi cama?
¿Has visto el anillo hipnótico que va de ojo a ojo
Del amor al amor del odio al odio
Del hombre a la mujer del planeta a la planeta?
¿Has visto en el cielo desierto
La paloma amenazada por los años
Con los ojos llenos de recuerdos
Con el pecho lleno de silencio
Más triste que el mar después de un naufragio?

Coming back from the time of the pharaohs?

Fear alters the form of the flowers
Who wait for the final judgment trembling
One by one the stars are launched from the balcony
The sea is falling asleep behind a tree
With its habitual calm
For it knows from biblical times
That return is unheard of on the pole-star

No navigator has ever met the rose of the seas
The rose that holds the memory of its ancestors
Deep within itself
Tired of dreaming
Tired of living in each petal
Wind you are thinking of the rose of the sea
I wait for you on foot at the end of this line
I know where it's hidden—the flower born of the sirens' sex
In moments of pleasure
When it starts to grow late beneath the sea
And the waves are heard rustling
Under the feet of the horizon
I know I know where it's hidden

The wind has the bee voice of a pale young woman
The young woman pale as her own statue
That I loved in a corner of my life
When I tried to leap from hope to heaven
And fell from shipwreck into shipwreck from horizon into horizon
Then I saw the self-hidden rose
No one had ever seen face to face

Have you seen this bird from faraway islands
Launched on the tide at the foot of my bed?
Have you seen the hypnotic ring that goes from eye to eye
From love to love from hate to hate
From man to woman from planet to planette?
Have you seen in the lonely sky
The dove menaced by the years
With eyes full of memories
A breast full of silence
Sadder than the sea after a shipwreck?

Detrás del águila postrera cantaba el cantador
Tenía un anillo en el corazón
Y se sentó en la tierra de su esfuerzo
Frente al volcán desafiado por una flor
El atleta quisiera ser un faro
Para tener barcos que lo miren
Para hacerlos dormir para dormirse
Y arrullar al cielo como un árbol
El atleta
Tiene un anillo en la garganta
Y así se pasa el tiempo
Quieto quieto
Porque le están creciendo anémonas en el cerebro

Contempla al huérfano que se paró en su edad
Por culpa de los ríos que llevan poca agua
Por culpa de las montañas que no bajan
Crece crece dice el violoncelo
Como yo estoy creciendo
Como está creciendo la idea del suicidio en la bella jardinera
Crece pequeño zafiro más tierno que la angustia
En los ojos del pájaro quemado

Creceré creceré cuando crezca la ciudad
Cuando los peces se hayan bebido todo el mar
Los días pasados son caparazones de tortuga
Ahora tengo barcos en la memoria
Y los barcos se acercan día a día
Oigo un ladrido de perro que da la vuelta al mundo
En tres semanas
Y se muere en llegando

El corazón ha roto las amarras
A causa de los vientos
Y el niño está quedándose huérfano

Si el paisaje se hiciera paloma
Antes de la noche se lo comería el mar
Pero el mar está preparando un naufragio
Y tiene sus pensamientos por otros lados

Navío navío
Tienes la vida corta de un abanico

After the last eagle the singer was singing
He had a ring in his heart
And sat down on the land of his spirit
Facing the volcano threatened by a flower
The athlete would like to be a lighthouse
To take the boats that look at him
And make them sleep so he can sleep
And coo at the sky like a tree
The athlete
Has a ring in his throat
And so he passes the time
Quiet quiet
Because anemones are growing in his brain

Study the orphan stopped in his tracks
By the sin of rivers bearing scant water
By the sin of mountains that won't bend down
Grow grow says the cello
Like I am growing
Like the idea of suicide grows in the beautiful gardener
A small sapphire softer than anguish grows
In the eyes of the burned bird

I'll grow I'll grow when the city grows
When the fish have drunk up all the sea
The past days are like turtle shells
Now I have boats in my memory
And the boats get closer day by day
I hear a dog's bark that turns the world around
In three weeks
And it's dead on arrival

The heart has broken its moorings
Because of the winds
And the child is staying an orphan

If the countryside became a dove
Before nightfall it would eat up the sea
But the sea is preparing a shipwreck
And its thoughts are occupied elsewhere

Ship ship
Your life short as the wave of a fan

Aquí nos reímos de todo eso
Aquí en el lejos lejos

La montaña embrujada por un ruiseñor
Sigue la miel del oso envenenado
Pobre oso de piel de oso envenenado por la noche boreal
Huye que huye de la muerte
De la muerte sentada al borde del mar

La montaña y el montaño
Con su luno y con su luna
La flor florecida y el flor floreciendo
Una flor que llaman girasol
Y un sol que se llama giraflor

El pájaro puede olvidar que es pájaro
A causa del cometa que no viene
Por miedo al invierno o a un atentado
El cometa que debía nacer de un telescopio y una hortensia
Que se creyó mirar y era mirado

Un aviador se mata sobre el concierto único
Y el ángel que se baña en algún piano
Se vuelve otra vez envuelto en sones
Buscando el receptor en los picachos
Donde brotan las palabras y los ríos

Los lobos hacen milagros
En las huellas de la noche
Cuando el pájaro incógnito se nubla
Y pastan las ovejas al otro lado de la luna

Si es un recuerdo de música
Nadie puede impedir que el circo se agrande en el silencio
Ni las campanas de los astros muertos
Ni la serpiente que se nutre de colores
Ni el pianista que está saliendo de la tierra
Ni el misionero que olvidó su nombre

Si el camino se sienta a descansar
O se remoja en el otoño de las constelaciones
Nadie impedirá que un alfiler se clave en la eternidad
Ni la mujer espolvoreada de mariposas

Here we laugh about all that
Here in the far far away

The mountain bewitched by a nightingale
Follows the honey of the poisoned bear
Poor bear with his bearskin poisoned by the northern night
Run run from death
From death sedate at the edge of the sea

Mr & mrs mountain
With her moon and with his moon
The flowered flower and the flower flowering
A flower they call sunflower
And a sun called flowersun

The bird can forget it's a bird
Because of the comet that never comes
For fear of the winter or of a crime
The comet that should have been born from a telescope and
    a hydrangea
That thought it would look but was being looked at

An aviator kills himself above the only concert
And the angel bathing in some piano
Turns around again wrapped in sound
Looking for the receiver at the summit
Where words and rivers emerge

The wolves make miracles
In the tracks of the night
When the unknown bird clouds over
And the sheep graze on the other side of the moon

If there's a hint of music
No one can stop the circus from expanding in the silence
Or the bells of the dead stars
Or the serpent who feeds on colors
Or the pianist who is rising from the earth
Or the missionary who forgot his name

If the road sits down to rest
Or soaks in the autumn of the constellations
No one will stop a pin from nailing itself in eternity
Or the woman powdered with butterflies

Ni el huérfano amaestrado por una tulipa
Ni la cebra que trota alrededor de un valse
Ni el guardián de la suerte

El cielo tiene miedo de la noche
Cuando el mar hace dormir los barcos
Cuando la muerte se nutre en los rincones
Y la voz del silencio se llena de vampiros
Entonces alumbramos un fuego bajo el oráculo
Para aplacar la suerte
Y alimentamos los milagros de la soledad
Con nuestra propia carne
Entonces en el cementerio sellado
Y hermoso como un eclipse
La rosa rompe sus lazos y florece al reverso de la muerte

Noche de viejos terrores de noche
¿En dónde está la gruta polar nutrida de milagros?
¿En dónde está el miraje delirante
De los ojos de arco iris y de la nebulosa?
Se abre la tumba y al fondo se ve el mar
El aliento se corta y el vértigo suspenso
Hincha las sienes se derrumba en las venas
Abre los ojos más grandes que el espacio que cabe en ellos
Y un grito se cicatriza en el vacío enfermo
Se abre la tumba y al fondo se ve un rebaño perdido en la montaña
La pastora con su capa de viento al lado de la noche
Cuenta las pisadas de Dios en el espacio
Y se canta a sí misma
Se abre la tumba y al fondo se ve un desfile de témpanos de hielo
Que brillan bajo los reflectores de la tormenta
Y pasan en silencio a la deriva
Solemne procesión de témpanos
Con hachones de luz dentro del cuerpo
Se abre la tumba y al fondo se ven el otoño y el invierno
Baja lento lento un cielo de amatista
Se abre la tumba y al fondo se ve una enorme herida
Que se agranda en lo profundo de la tierra
Con un ruido de verano y primaveras
Se abre la tumba y al fondo se ve una selva de hadas que se fecundan
Cada árbol termina en un pájaro extasiado

Or the orphan schooled by a tulip
Or the zebra trotting around a waltz
Or the guardian of fate

The sky is afraid of the night
When the sea puts the boats to sleep
When death fattens on corners
And the voice of silence is full of vampires
Then we light a fire under the oracle
To pacify fate
And we feed the miracles of solitude
With our own flesh
Then in the cemetery sealed
And beautiful as an eclipse
The rose breaks its chains and blooms on the other side of death

Night of the old night terrors
Where is the polar cavern abounding in miracles?
Where is the raving mirage
Of misty and rainbow eyes?
The tomb is opened revealing at bottom the sea
Breath is severed and vertigo hangs suspended
It swells the temples crumbles the veins
It opens the eyes wider than the space contained within them
And a scream heals itself in the sick vacancy
The tomb is opened revealing a flock lost on the mountain
The shepherdess with her cape of wind beside the night
Counts the footprints of God in space
And sings to herself
The tomb is opened revealing a marching of icebergs
That glow beneath the searchlights of the storm
And a solemn procession of blocks
With torches of light inside their bodies
Passes drifting in silence
The tomb is opened revealing the fall and the winter
Slowly slowly an amethyst heaven descends
The tomb is opened revealing an enormous wound
That is spreading into the depths of the earth
With a noise of summer and springs
The tomb is opened revealing a forest of self-fertilizing fairies
Every tree is topped by an ecstatic bird

Y todo queda adentro de la elipse cerrada de sus cantos
Por esos lados debe hallarse el nido de las lágrimas
Que ruedan por el cielo y cruzan el zodíaco
De signo en signo
Se abre la tumba y al fondo se ve la hirviente nebulosa que se apaga
　y se alumbra
Un aerolito pasa sin responder a nadie
Danzan luminarias en el cadalso ilimitado
En donde las cabezas sangrientas de los astros
Dejan un halo que crece eternamente
Se abre la tumba y salta una ola
La sombra del universo se salpica
Y todo lo que vive en la sombra o en la orilla
Se abre la tumba y sale un sollozo de planetas
Hay mástiles tronchados y remolinos de naufragios
Doblan las campanas de todas las estrellas
Silba el huracán perseguido a través del infinito
Sobre los ríos desbordados
Se abre la tumba y salta un ramo de flores cargadas de cilicios
Crece la hoguera impenetrable y un olor de pasión invade el orbe
El sol tantea el último rincón donde se esconde
Y nace la selva mágica
Se abre la tumba y al fondo se ve el mar
Sube un canto de mil barcos que se van
En tanto un tropel de peces
Se petrifica lentamente

Cuánto tiempo ese dedo de silencio
Dominando el insomnio interminable
Que reina en las esferas
Es hora de dormir en todas partes
El sueño saca al hombre de la tierra

Festejamos el amanecer con las ventanas
Festejamos el amanecer con los sombreros
Se vuela el terror del cielo
Los cerros se lanzan pájaros a la cara
Amanecer con esperanza de aeroplanos
Bajo la bóveda que cuela la luz desde tantos siglos
Amor y paciencia de columna central

And all remains inside the ellipse locked within its songs
By those directions one should find the nest of tears
That roll through heaven and cruise the zodiac
From sign to sign
The tomb is opened revealing the seething fog turning off and on
A meteorite goes by without answering anyone
Votive lights dance on the boundless scaffold
Where the bloody heads of the stars
Leave a halo that grows eternally
The tomb is opened and out leaps a wave
The shadow of the universe splashes itself
And everything that lives in the shade or on the shore
The tomb is opened and a planetary sob escapes
Among the lopped-off masts and shipwreck whirlpools
The bells of all the stars toll
The hurricane whistles harassed across infinity
Over spilled-over rivers
The tomb is opened and a branch of flowers leaps out loaded with
    hairshirts
The impenetrable bonfire grows and an odor of passion invades the orb
The sun sketches the last corner to hide itself
And the magic forest is born
The tomb is opened revealing at bottom the sea
A song rises from a thousand outgoing ships
Meanwhile a rush of fish
Is petrifying slowly

For ages now that finger of silence
Dominating the endless insomnia
That rules throughout the spheres
Everywhere it's time to sleep
Sleep takes man from the earth

We woo the dawn with windows
We woo the dawn with hats
The terror of heaven is flying
Hills are throwing birds in our faces
Dawn with the hope of aeroplanes
Under the vault that filters light from so many ages
Central column of love and patience

Nos frotamos las manos y reímos
Nos lavamos los ojos y jugamos

El horizonte es un rinoceronte
El mar un azar
El cielo un pañuelo
La llaga una plaga
Un horizonte jugando a todo mar se sonaba con el cielo después de las
siete llagas de Egipto
El rinoceronte navega sobre el azar como el cometa en su pañuelo lleno
de plagas

Razón del día no es razón de noche
Y cada tiempo tiene insinuación distinta
Los vegetales salen a comer al borde
Las olas tienden las manos
Para coger un pájaro
Todo es variable en el mirar sencillo
Y en los subterráneos de la vida
Tal vez sea lo mismo

La herida de luna de la pobre loca
La pobre loca de la luna herida
Tenía luz en la celeste boca
Boca celeste que la luz tenía
El mar de flor para esperanza ciega
Ciega esperanza para flor de mar
Cantar para el ruiseñor que al cielo pega
Pega el cielo al ruiseñor para cantar

Jugamos fuera del tiempo
Y juega con nosotros el molino de viento
Molino de viento
Molino de aliento
Molino de cuento
Molino de intento
Molino de aumento
Molino de ungüento
Molino de sustento
Molino de tormento
Molino de salvamento
Molino de advenimiento

We rub our hands and laugh
We wash our eyes and play

> The horizon is a rhinoceros
> The sea unlucky
> Heaven a hanky
> The dirge a scourge

A horizon playing at sea blows its nose with heaven after the seven
    dirges of Egypt
The rhinoceros sails over the unlucky like a comet on its hanky full of
    scourges

The day's reason is not the night's
And every time has a distinct insinuation
The plants come out to eat the border
The waves stretch their hands
To catch a bird
All is variable in simple seeing
And down in the caverns of life
Perhaps it's the same

The moon wound of the poor mad woman
The poor mad woman of the wounded moon
Had light in her heavenly mouth
Heavenly mouth the light had
The flower sea for blind hope
Blind hope for the sea flower
Singing for the nightingale that joins heaven
Join heaven to the nightingale for singing

We play outside time
And the windmill plays with us
Mill of wind
Mill of breath
Mill of story
Mill of purpose
Mill of growth
Mill of ointment
Mill of food
Mill of torture
Mill of safety
Mill of arrival

Molino de tejimiento
Molino de rugimiento
Molino de tañimiento
Molino de afletamiento
Molino de agolpamiento
Molino de alargamiento
Molino de alejamiento
Molino de amasamiento
Molino de engendramiento
Molino de ensoñamiento
Molino de ensalzamiento
Molino de enterramiento
Molino de maduramiento
Molino de malogramiento
Molino de maldecimiento
Molino de sacudimiento
Molino de revelamiento
Molino de obscurecimiento
Molino de enajenamiento
Molino de enamoramiento
Molino de encabezamiento
Molino de encastillamiento
Molino de aparecimiento
Molino de despojamiento
Molino de atesoramiento
Molino de enloquecimiento
Molino de ensortijamiento
Molino de envenenamiento
Molino de acontecimiento
Molino de descuartizamiento
Molino del portento
Molino del lamento
Molino del momento
Molino del firmamento
Molino del sentimiento
Molino del juramento
Molino del ardimiento
Molino del crecimiento
Molino del nutrimiento
Molino del conocimiento

Mill of weaving
Mill of roaring
Mill of ringing
Mill of farting
Mill of heaping
Mill of elongating
Mill of retiring
Mill of massaging
Mill of begetting
Mill of fantasy
Mill of praise
Mill of burial
Mill of ripening
Mill of failing
Mill of slander
Mill of shock
Mill of revelation
Mill of obscuration
Mill of insanity
Mill of loving
Mill of headcounting
Mill of encastling
Mill of appearance
Mill of stripping
Mill of hoarding
Mill of goingmad
Mill of curling
Mill of poisoning
Mill of happening
Mill of piecing
Mill of the portent
Mill of the lament
Mill of the moment
Mill of the firmament
Mill of the sentiment
Mill of the curse
Mill of the valorous
Mill of the increase
Mill of the nourishing
Mill of the knowing

Molino del descendimiento
Molino del desollamiento
Molino del elevamiento
Molino del endiosamiento
Molino del alumbramiento
Molino del deliramiento
Molino del aburrimiento
Molino del engreimiento
Molino del escalamiento
Molino del descubrimiento
Molino del escurrimiento
Molino del remordimiento
Molino del redoblamiento
Molino del atronamiento
Molino del aturdimiento
Molino del despeñamiento
Molino del quebrantamiento
Molino del envejecimiento
Molino del aceleramiento
Molino del encarnizamiento
Molino del anonadamiento
Molino del arrepentimiento
Molino del encanecimiento
Molino del despedazamiento
Molino del descorazonamiento
Molino en fragmento
Molino en detrimento
Molino en giramiento
Molino en gruñimiento
Molino en sacramento
Molino en pensamiento
Molino en pulsamiento
Molino en pudrimiento
Molino en nacimiento
Molino en apiñamiento
Molino en apagamiento
Molino en decaimiento
Molino en derretimiento
Molino en desvalimiento
Molino en marchitamiento

Mill of the lowering
Mill of the fleecing
Mill of the ecstasy
Mill of the loftiness
Mill of the illuminating
Mill of the raving
Mill of the boring
Mill of the vanity
Mill of the scaling
Mill of the finding
Mill of the dripping
Mill of the regretting
Mill of the redoubling
Mill of the dumbfounding
Mill of the giddiness
Mill of the runs
Mill of the break-in
Mill of the aging
Mill of the hastening
Mill of the fleshing
Mill of the annihilating
Mill of the repentance
Mill of the meagreness
Mill of the mangling
Mill of the disheartening
Mill in fragment
Mill in detriment
Mill in whirling
Mill in growling
Mill in sacrament
Mill in thought
Mill in pulsing
Mill in rotting
Mill in birthing
Mill in crowding
Mill in quenching
Mill in decaying
Mill in languishing
Mill in dereliction
Mill in withering

Molino en enfadamiento
Molino en encantamiento
Molino en transformamiento
Molino en asolamiento
Molino en concebimiento
Molino en derribamiento
Molino en imaginamiento
Molino en desamparamiento
Molino con talento
Molino con acento
Molino con sufrimiento
Molino con temperamento
Molino con fascinamiento
Molino con hormigamiento
Molino con retorcimiento
Molino con resentimiento
Molino con refregamiento
Molino con recogimiento
Molino con razonamiento
Molino con quebrantamiento
Molino con prolongamiento
Molino con presentimiento
Molino con padecimiento
Molino con amordazamiento
Molino con enronquecimiento
Molino con alucinamiento
Molino con atolondramiento
Molino con desfallecimiento
Molino para aposento
Molino para convento
Molino para ungimiento
Molino para alojamiento
Molino para cargamento
Molino para subimento
Molino para flotamiento
Molino para enfriamiento
Molino para embrujamiento
Molino para acogimiento
Molino para apostamiento
Molino para arrobamiento

Mill in angering
Mill in enchanting
Mill in transforming
Mill in destroying
Mill in conceiving
Mill in demolishing
Mill in imagining
Mill in abandoning
Mill with talent
Mill with accent
Mill with patience
Mill with temperament
Mill with fascination
Mill with ant-itch
Mill with contortion
Mill with grudge
Mill with friction
Mill with collection
Mill with reason
Mill with rupture
Mill with prolongation
Mill with presentiment
Mill with sufferance
Mill with muzzle
Mill with hoarseness
Mill with hallucination
Mill with amazement
Mill with languor
Mill for apartment
Mill for convent
Mill for unction
Mill for lodging
Mill for cargo
Mill for rising
Mill for floating
Mill for chilling
Mill for bewitching
Mill for welcoming
Mill for betting
Mill for bliss

Molino para escapamiento
Molino para escondimiento
Molino para estrellamiento
Molino para exaltamiento
Molino para guarecimiento
Molino para levantamiento
Molino para machucamiento
Molino para renovamiento
Molino para desplazamiento
Molino para anticipamiento
Molino para amonedamiento
Molino para profetizamiento
Molino para descoyuntamiento
Molino como ornamento
Molino como elemento
Molino como armamento
Molino como instrumento
Molino como monumento
Molino como palpamiento
Molino como descubrimiento
Molino como anunciamiento
Molino como medicamento
Molino como desvelamiento
Molino a sotavento
Molino a barlovento
Molino a ligamento
Molino a lanzamiento
Molino a mordimiento
Molino a movimiento
Molino que invento
Molino que ahuyento
Molino que oriento
Molino que caliento
Molino que presiento
Molino que apaciento
Molino que transparento
Molino lento
Molino cruento
Molino atento
Molino hambriento
Molino sediento

Mill for escape
Mill for concealment
Mill for starriness
Mill for exaltation
Mill for sheltering
Mill for uprising
Mill for pounding
Mill for reforming
Mill for displacement
Mill for anticipation
Mill for coining
Mill for prophecy
Mill for dislocation
Mill as ornament
Mill as element
Mill as armament
Mill as instrument
Mill as monument
Mill as touching
Mill as discovery
Mill as announcement
Mill as medicine
Mill as watchfulness
Mill to leeward
Mill to windward
Mill to chain
Mill to launch
Mill to bite
Mill to move
Mill I invent
Mill I banish
Mill I orient
Mill I heat
Mill I foresee
Mill I shinethrough
Slow mill
Cruel mill
Polite mill
Hungry mill
Thirsty mill

Molino sangriento
Molino jumento
Molino violento
Molino contento
Molino opulento
Molino friolento
Molino avariento
Molino corpulento
Molino achaquiento
Molino granujiento
Molino ceniciento
Molino polvoriento
Molino cazcarriento
Molino gargajiento
Molino sudoriento
Molino macilento
Molino soñoliento
Molino turbulento
Molino truculento

Así eres molino de viento
Molino de asiento
Molino de asiento del viento
Que teje las noches y las mañanas
Que hila las nieblas de ultratumba
Molino de aspavientos y del viento en aspas
El paisaje se llena de tus locuras

Y el trigo viene y va
De la tierra al cielo
Del cielo al mar
Los trigos de las olas amarillas
Donde el viento se revuelca
Buscando la cosquilla de las espigas

Escucha
Pasa el palpador en eléctricas corrientes
El viento norte despeina tus cabellos
Hurra molino moledor
Molino volador
Molino charlador

Bloody mill
Ass mill
Violent mill
Content mill
Opulent mill
Chilly mill
Miserly mill
Fatty mill
Sickly mill
Pimply mill
Ashen mill
Dusty mill
Muddy mill
Spitting mill
Sweating mill
Skinny mill
Lazy mill
Turbulent mill
Truculent mill

So you're a windmill
A millstone
A windmillstone that
Weaves together nights and mornings
Spins the fog beyond the grave
Mill blown through and overblown
The landscape overflows with your follies

And the wheat comes and goes
From earth to heaven
From heaven to sea
The yellow waves of wheat
Where the wind wallows
Inviting a tickling from the ears

Listen
The pulsar passes in electric currents
The north wind musses your hair
Hurray grinding mill
Flying mill
Chatter mill

Molino cantador
Cuando el cielo trae de la mano una tempestad
Hurra molino girando en la memoria
Molino que hipnotiza las palomas viajeras

Habla habla molino de cuento
Cuando el viento narra tu leyenda etérea
Sangra sangra molino del descendimiento
Con tu gran recuerdo pegado a los ocasos del mundo
Y los brazos de tu cruz fatigados por el huracán

Así reímos y cantamos en esta hora
Porque el molino ha creado el imperio de su luz escogida
Y es necesario que lo sepa
Es necesario que alguien se lo diga

Sol tú que naciste en mi ojo derecho
Y moriste en mi ojo izquierdo
No creas en los vaticinios del zodíaco
Ni en los ladridos de las tumbas
Las tumbas tienen maleficios de luna
Y no saben lo que hablan

Yo te lo digo porque mi sombrero está cansado de recorrer el mundo
Y tengo una experiencia de mariposa milenaria

Profetiza profetiza
Molino de las constelaciones
Mientras bailamos sobre el azar de la risa
Ahora que la grúa que nos trae el día
Volcó la noche fuera de la tierra

Empiece ya
La farandolina en la lejantaña de la montanía
El horimento bajo el firmazonte
Se embarca en la luna
Para dar la vuelta al mundo
Empiece ya
La faranmandó mandó liná
Con su musiquí con su musicá

La carabantantina
La carabantantú
La farandosilina

Singing mill
When the sky brings a storm by hand
Hurray mill whirling in memory
Hypnotizing the carrier pigeons

Speak speak mill of story
When the wind recites your ethereal legend
Bleed bleed mill of descent
With your grand memento stuck to the sunsets of the world
And the arms of your cross tired out by the hurricane

So this is the hour we laugh and sing
Because the mill created its empire of chosen light
And it must be known
Someone must say it

Sun you who were born in my right eye
And died in my left eye
Don't believe in predictions from the zodiac
Or in barks from the tombs
The tombs are full of moon spells
And don't know what they're saying

I tell you because my hat is tired of roaming the world
And I'm having a millennial butterfly experience

Prophesy prophesy
Mill of the constellations
While we dance upon the laugh's accident
Now that the crane that scoops us the day
Tossed the night right out of the earth

Begin now
The farandolina in the distain of the mountance
The horiment under the firmazon
Sails away on the moon
To turn the world around
Begin now
The faranmandó mandó liná
With its musiquí with its musicá

The carabantantina
The carabantantú
The farandosilina

La Farandú
La Carabantantá
La Carabantí
La fanrandosilá
La faransí

Ríe ríe antes que venga la fatiga
En su carro nebuloso de días
Y los años y los siglos
Se amontonen en el vacío
Y todo sea oscuro en el ojo del cielo

La cascada que cabellera sobre la noche
Mientras la noche se cama a descansar
Con su luna que almohada al cielo
Yo ojo el paisaje cansado
Que se ruta hacia el horizonte
A la sombra de un árbol naufragando

Y he aquí que ahora me diluyo en múltiples cosas
Soy luciérnaga y voy iluminando las ramas de la selva
Sin embargo cuando vuelo guardo mi modo de andar
Y no sólo soy luciérnaga
Sino también el aire en que vuela
La luna me atraviesa de parte a parte
Dos pájaros se pierden en mi pecho
Sin poderlo remediar
Y luego soy árbol
Y en cuanto a árbol conservo mis modos de luciérnaga
Y mis modos de cielo
Y mi andar de hombre mi triste andar
Ahora soy rosal y hablo con lenguaje de rosal
Y digo
Sal rosa rorosalía
Sal rosa al día
Salía al sol rosa sario
Fueguisa mía sonrodería rososoro oro
Ando pequeño volcán del día
Y tengo miedo del volcán
Mas el volcán responde
Prófugo rueda al fondo donde ronco
Soy rosa de trueno y sueno mis carrasperas

The Farandú
The Carabantantá
The Carabantantí
The farandosilá
The faransí

Laugh laugh before weariness comes
In his cloudy car of days
And the years and the ages
Pile up in the void
And all is dark in the eye of heaven

The cascade that longhairs over the night
While the night beds to lie down
With its moon that pillows at the sky
I eye the tired countryside
That routes toward heaven
At the shade of a stranding tree

Here and now I have to dilute myself into many things
I am firefly and I go lighting the boughs of the forest
However when I fly I watch the way I move
And I'm not only firefly
But also the air it flies on
The moon passes over me from one side to the other
Two birds are lost in my breast
And they can't help it
And soon I'm a tree
And while a tree I keep my firefly ways
And my sky ways
And my human movement my sad walking
Now I'm rosebush and speak in rosebush language
And I say
Rise rose rorosarose
Rise rose to the day
Rose ary arose to the sun
My fireling smilerounding rosesore ore
I move into the day's volcano
And I'm afraid of volcanos
But the volcano replies
Fugitive roller at the depths where I snore
I'm rose of thunder sounding my hoarse voice

Estoy preso y arrastro mis propios grillos
Los astros que trago crujen en mis entrañas
Proa a la borrasca en procesión procreadora
Proclamo mis proezas bramadoras
Y mis bronquios respiran en la tierra profounda
Bajo los mares y las montañas
Y luego soy pájaro
Y me disputo el día en gorjeos
El día que me cruza la garganta
Ahora solamente digo
Callaos que voy a cantar
Soy el único cantor de este siglo
Mío mío es todo el infinito
Mis mentiras huelen a cielo
Y nada más
Y ahora soy mar
Pero guardo algo de mis modos de volcán
De mis modos de árbol de mis modos de luciérnaga
De mis modos de pájaro de hombre y de rosal
Y hablo como mar y digo
De la firmeza hasta el horicielo
Soy todo montalas en la azulaya
Bailo en las volaguas con espurinas
Una corriela tras de la otra
Ondola en olañas mi rugazuleo
Las verdondilas bajo la luna del selviflujo
Van en montonda hasta el infidondo
Y cuando bramuran los hurafones
Y la ondaja lanza a las playas sus laziolas
Hay un naufundo que grita pidiendo auxilio
Yo me hago el sordo
Miro las butraceas lentas sobre mis tornadelas
La subaterna con sus brajidos
Las escalolas de la montasca
Las escalolas de la desonda
Que no descansan hasta que roen el borde de los altielos
Hasta que llegan al abifunda
En tanto el pirata canta
Y yo lo escucho vestido de verdiul

I'm a prisoner dragging my own irons
The stars I swallow sizzle my guts
Prow to the storm in procreative procession
I proclaim my roaring prowess
And my bronchials breathe in the deep earth
Under the seas and the mountains
And then I'm bird
And I argue all day in chirps
The day my throat comes across me
I alone will say
Be quiet I'm going to sing
I am this age's only singer
Mine mine is all the infinite
My lies smell of heaven
And nothing else
And now I'm sea
But I keep some of my volcano ways
Of my tree ways of my firefly ways
Of my bird ways of man and of rosebush
And I speak like sea and I say
From the firmahead to the horisky
I'm all mountwings on the blueach
I dance on the soarwaters with swalloams
One glimmerun after the other
Swellave on wavetain my blueripplish
The greenfinches under the moon of the flowood
Rise in mountwave toward the infiround
And when the huraphoons haulroar
And the lowave throws its lassowaves at the coast
There's a shipdeep cries pleading for help
I become deaf
I look at the slow traptraces over my backtracks
The sublighthouse with its bellowmoos
The stairwaves of the stormount
The stairwaves of the swellow
That won't rest until they eat away the border of higheaven
Until they reach the opundity
Meanwhile the pirate sings
And I listen dressed in veridue

La lona en el mar riela
En la luna gime el viento
Y alza en blanco crujimiento
Alas de olas en mi azul

El mar se abrirá para dejar salir los primeros náufragos
Que cumplieron su castigo
Después de tantos siglos y más siglos
Andarán por la tierra con miradas de vidrio
Escalarán los montes de sus frases proféticas
Y se convertirán en constelaciones
Entonces aparecerá un volcán en medio de las olas
Y dirá yo soy el rey
Traedme el armonio de las nebulosas
Y sabed que las islas son las coronas de mi cabeza
Y las olas mi único tesoro
Yo soy el rey
El rey canta a la reina
El cielo canta a la ciela
El luz canta a la luz
La luz que busca el ojo hasta que lo encuentra
Canta el cielo en su lengua astronómica
Y la luz en su idioma magnético
Mientras el mar lame los pies de la reina
Que se peina eternamente
Yo soy el rey
Y os digo que el planeta que atravesó la noche
No se reconoce al salir por el otro lado
Y mucho menos al entrar en el día
Pues ni siquiera recuerda cómo se llamaba
Ni quiénes eran sus padres
Dime ¿eres hijo de Martín Pescador
O eres nieto de una cigüeña tartamuda
O de aquella jirafa que vi en medio del desierto
Pastando ensimismada las yerbas de la luna
O eres hijo del ahorcado que tenía ojos de pirámide?
Algún día lo sabremos
Y morirás sin tu secreto
Y de tu tumba saldrá un arco iris como un tranvía
Del arco iris saldrá una pareja haciendo el amor
Del amor saldrá una selva errante

The sail in the sea shimmers
On the moon the wind moans
And heaves in white creaking
Wings of waves in my blue

The sea will open to free the first of the shipwrecked
Who fulfilled their punishment
After so many ages and more ages
They will walk on the land with glances of glass
They will scale the mountains of their prophetic phrases
And be transformed into constellations
Then will appear a volcano in the midst of the waves
And it will say I am king
Bring me the harmonium of the misties
And know that the islands are the crowns on my head
And the waves my only treasure
I am king
The king sings to the queen
The sky sings to the skye
The leit sings to the light
The light who looks for the eye until she finds it
The sky sings in his astronomical tongue
And the light in her magnetic idiom
While the sea laps at the feet of the queen
Who does her hair endlessly
I am king
And I tell you the planet who crossed the night
Doesn't know himself when he pops through the other side
Much less when he enters the day
He doesn't even remember his name
Or who his parents were
Tell me are you the son of Fisher Martin
Or are you grandson of a stuttering stork
Or of that giraffe I see in the middle of the desert
Selfishly grazing on moon grass
Or are you the son of the hanged man who had pyramid eyes?
One day we'll know
And you'll die without your secret
And from your tomb will spring a rainbow like a bus
From the rainbow will spring a couple making love
From the love will spring a roving forest

De la selva saldrá una flecha
De la flecha saldrá una liebre huyendo por los campos
De la liebre saldrá una cinta que irá señalando su camino
De la cinta saldrá un río y una catarata que salvará a la liebre de sus
    perseguidores
Hasta que la liebre empiece a trepar por una mirada
Y se esconda al fondo del ojo

Yo soy el rey
Los ahogados florecen cuando yo lo mando
Atad el arco iris al pirata
Atad el viento a los cabellos de la bruja
Yo soy el rey
Y trazaré tu horóscopo como un plan de batalla

Oyendo esto el arco iris se alejaba
¿A dónde vas arco iris
No sabes que hay asesinos en todos los caminos?
El iris encadenado en la columna montante
Columna de mercurio en fiesta para nosotros
Tres mil doscientos metros de infrarojo
Un extremo se apoya en mi pie y el otro en la llaga de Cristo
Los domingos del arco iris para el arcángel
¿En dónde está el arquero de los meteoros?
El arquero arcaico
Bajo la arcada eterna el arquero del arcano con su violín violeta con su
    violín violáceo con su violín violado
Arco iris arco de las cejas en mi cielo arqueológico
Bajo el área del arco se esconde el arca de tesoros preciosos
Y la flor montada como un reloj
Con el engranaje perfecto de sus pétalos
Ahora que un caballo empieza a subir galopando por el arco iris
Ahora la mirada descarga los ojos demasiado llenos
En el instante en que huyen los ocasos a través de las llanuras
El cielo está esperando un aeroplano
Y yo oigo la risa de los muertos debajo de la tierra

From the forest will spring an arrow
From the arrow will spring a hare fleeing through the fields
From the hare will spring a ribbon to go marking its way
From the ribbon will spring a river and a waterfall that will save the
    hare from its pursuers
Until the hare begins to creep through a glance
And climbs to the bottom of the eye

I am king
The drowned flower when I command it
Tie the rainbow to the pirate
Tie the wind to the witch's hair
I am king
And I will trace your horoscope like a battle plan

Hearing this the rainbow edged away
Where are you going rainbow
Don't you know murderers lurk on every road?
The rainbow chained in the upright column
Column of mercury on holiday for us
Three thousand two hundred meters of infrared
One end leans on my foot and the other on the wound of Christ
The rainbow's Sundays for the archangel
Where is the archer of the meteors?
The archaic archer
Under the eternal arcade the archer of the arcanum with his violet
    violin with his violaceous violin with his violin violated
Rainbow arch of eyebrows in my archeological sky
Under the area of the arch is hidden the ark of precious treasure
And the flower mounted as a clock
With the perfect gears of its petals
Just now a horse begins to gallop up the rainbow
Now the glance unloads the swollen eyes
At the moment when the sunsets flee across the plains
The sky is looking for an aeroplane
And I hear the laughter of the dead beneath the earth   [S.F.]

CANTO VI

Alhaja apoteosis y molusco
Anudado
      noche
          nudo
El corazón
Esa entonces dirección
          nudo temblando
Flexible corazón la apoteosis
Un dos tres
      cuatro
Lágrima
      mi lámpara
          y molusco
El pecho al melodioso
Anudado la joya
Conque temblando angustia
Normal tedio
      Sería pasión
      Muerte el violoncelo
Una bujía el ojo
      Otro otra
Cristal si cristal era
Cristaleza
Magnetismo
      sabéis la seda
Viento flor
      lento nube lento
Seda cristal lento seda
El magnetismo
      seda aliento cristal seda
Así viajando en postura de ondulación
Cristal nube
Molusco sí por violoncelo y joya
Muerte de joya y violoncelo
Así sed por hambre o hambre y sed
Y nube y joya
Lento
      nube

CANTO VI

Gemstone apotheosis and mollusk
Knotted
       night
          node
The heart
That then direction
                trembling node
Flexible heart the apotheosis
One two three
          four
Lament
      my lamp
           and mollusk
The breast goes melodious
Knotted the jewel
So then anguish trembling
Normal tedium
            Could be passion
            Death the cello
A candle the eye
            Other another
Crystal if crystal it was
Crystalness
Magnetism
         you know the silk
Wind flower
         slow cloud slow
Silk crystal slow silk
The magnetism
         silk breath crystal silk
Thus traveling in posture of undulation
Crystal cloud
Mollusk itself for cello and jewel
Death of jewel and cello
So thirst for hunger or hunger and thirst
And cloud and jewel
Slow
      cloud

Ala ola ole ala Aladino
El ladino Aladino Ah ladino dino la
Cristal nube
Adónde
    en dónde
Lento lenta
      ala ola
Ola ola el ladino si ladino
Pide ojos
      Tengo nácar
En la seda cristal nube
Cristal ojos
      y perfumes
Bella tienda
Cristal nube
      muerte joya o en ceniza
Porque eterno porque eterna
          lento lenta
Al azar del cristal ojos
Gracia tanta
      y entre mares
Miramares
Nombres daba
      por los ojos hojas mago
Alto alto
Y el clarín de la Babel
Pida nácar
      tenga muerte
Una dos y cuatro muerte
Para el ojo y entre mares
Para el barco en los perfumes
Por la joya al infinito
Vestir cielo sin desmayo
Se deshoja tan prodigio
El cristal ojo
Y la visita
      flor y rama
Al gloria trino
        apoteosis
Va viajando Nudo Noche

Ala ola ole ala Aladino
El ladino Aladino Ah ladino dino la
Crystal cloud
Whither
              wherein
Linger longer
                    wing wave
Wave wave the knave if knave
Plead for eyes
                    I've mother-of-pearl
In the silk crystal cloud
Crystal eyes
                    and perfumes
Lovely store
Crystal cloud
                    death jewel or in ash
Because eternal because eternelle
                                   linger longer
On the hazard of crystal eyes
So much grace
                    and among seas
Seaviews
Names he gave
                    for the eyes leaves Magus
High high
And Babel's trumpet
Begs mother-of-pearl
                    has death
One two and four death
For the eye and among seas
For the ship in the perfumes
Through the jewel to infinity
To cloak heaven without dismay
Strips itself such wonder
The crystal eye
And the visitor
                    flower and branch
To triune gloria
                    apotheosis
Goes traveling Node Night

Me daría
        cristaleras
                tanto azar
                        y noche y noche
Que tenía la borrasca
Noche y noche
                Apoteosis
Que tenía cristal ojo cristal seda cristal nube
La escultura seda o noche
Lluvia
        Lana flor por ojo
                Flor por nube
                Flor por noche
Señor horizonte viene viene
Puerta
Iluminando negro
Puerta hacia idas estatuarias
Estatuas de aquella ternura
A dónde va
De dónde viene
                el paisaje viento seda
El paisaje
        señor verde
Quién diría
Que se iba
Quién diría cristal noche
Tanta tarde
Tanto cielo que levanta
Señor cielo
        cristal cielo
Y las llamas
        y en mi reino
Ancla noche apoteosis
Anudado
        la tormenta
Ancla cielo
        sus raíces
El destino tanto azar
Se desliza deslizaba
Apagándose pradera

Could give me
                glassmakers
                        mass hazard
                                and night and night
That held the storm
Night and night
                Apotheosis
That held crystal eye crystal silk crystal cloud
The sculpture silk or night
Rain
        Fleece flower for eye
                Flower for cloud
                Flower for night
Lord horizon comes is coming
Door
Illuminating black
Door toward statuary departures
Statues of that tenderness
Whither goes
Whence comes
                the landscape wind silk
The landscape
                lord green
Who could say
What is gone
Who could say crystal night
So much afternoon
So much heaven lifting
Lord heaven
                crystal heaven
And the flames
                and in my reign
Night anchors apotheosis
Knotted
        the torment
Anchors heaven
                its roots
Fate so much hazard
Is slipping was slipping
Pasture dying out

Por quien sueña
Lunancero cristal luna
En que sueña
En que reino
                    de sus hierros
Ancla mía golondrina
Sus resortes en el mar
Angel mío
              tan obscuro
                          tan color
Tan estatua y tan aliento
Tierra y mano
La marina tan armada
Armaduras los cabellos
Ojos templo
              y el mendigo
Estallado corazón
Montanario
Campañoso
Suenan perlas
Llaman perlas
El honor de los adioses
                          Cristal nube
El rumor y la lazada
Nadadora
              Cristal noche
La medusa irreparable
Dirá espectro
                    Cristal seda
Olvidando la serpiente
Olvidando sus dos piernas
Sus dos ojos
Sus dos manos
Sus orejas
Aeronauta
              en mi terror
Viento aparte
Mandodrina y golonlina
Mandolera y ventolina
Enterradas

Through whoever dreams
Mooningbook crystal moon
Wherein dreams
Where I rule
            from her fetters
My swallow anchors
Her springs in the sea
My angel
            so dark
                    so color
So statue and so breath
Earth and hand
The marines greatly armed
Armoring the hair
Eyes temple
            and the beggar
Heart exploded
Mountainary
Fieldish
Pearls ring
Pearls call
The honor of the good-byes
                            Crystal cloud
The rumor and the bow-knot
Swimmer
            Crystal night
The irreparable medusa
Will speak a spectre
                    Crystal silk
Forgetting the serpent
Forgetting its two legs
Its two eyes
Its two hands
Its ears
Aeronaut
            in my terror
Away wind
Mandolow and swalin
Mandoness and windilin
Buried

Las campanas
Enterrados los olvidos
En su oreja
        viento norte
Cristal mío
Baño eterno
        el nudo noche
El gloria trino
        sin desmayo
Al tan prodigio
Con su estatua
Noche y rama
        Cristal sueño
        Cristal viaje
Flor y noche
Con su estatua
        Cristal muerte

The bells
Buried the forgotten
In your ear
        north wind
My crystal
Bath eternal
        the node night
The triune gloria
        without dismay
To such a wonder
With its statue
Night and branch
        Crystal trip
        Crystal dream
Flower and night
With its statue
        Crystal death

[S.F.]

CANTO VII

Ai aia aia
ia ia ia aia ui
Tralalí
Lali lalá
Aruaru
    urulario
Lalilá
Rimbibolam lam lam
Uiaya zollonario
      lalilá
Monlutrella monluztrella
        lalolú
Montresol y mandotrina
Ai ai
    Montesur en lasurido
    Montesol
Lusponsedo solinario
Aururaro ulisamento lalilá
Ylarca murllonía
Hormajauma marijauda
Mitradente
Mitrapausa
Mitralonga
Matrisola
    matriola
Olamina olasica lalilá
Isonauta
Olandera uruaro
Ia ia campanuso compasedo
Tralalá
Ai ai mareciente y eternauta
Redontella tallerendo lucenario
Ia ia
Laribamba
Larimbambamplanerella
Laribambamositerella
Leiramombaririlanla
    lirilam

Ai i a
Temporía
Ai ai aia
Ululayu
      lulayu
            layu yu
Ululayu
      ulayu
            ayu yu
Lunatando
Sensorida e infimento
Ululayo ululamento
Plegasuena
Cantasorio ululaciente
Oraneva yu yu yo
Tempovío
Infilero e infinauta zurrosía
Jaurinario ururayú
Montañendo oraranía
Arorasía ululacente
Semperiva
          ivarisa tarirá
Campanudio lalalí
      Auriciento auronida
Lalalí
    Io ia
i i i o
Ai a i ai a i i i i o ia

Ver Y Palpar

To See and Feel

1941

FUERZAS NATURALES

Una mirada
                    para abatir al albatros
Dos miradas
                    para detener el paisaje
                    al borde del río
Tres miradas
                    para cambiar la niña en
                    volantín
Cuatro miradas
                    para sujetar el tren que
                    cae en abismo
Cinco miradas
                    para volver a encender las estrellas
                    apagadas por el huracán
Seis miradas
                    para impedir el nacimiento
                    del niño acuático
Siete miradas
                    para prolongar la vida de
                    la novia
Ocho miradas
                    para cambiar el mar
                    en cielo
Nueve miradas
                    para hacer bailar los
                    árboles del bosque
Diez miradas
                    para ver la belleza que se presenta
                    entre un sueño y una catástrofe

NATURALEZA VIVA

El deja al acordeón el fin del mundo
Paga con la lluvia la última canción
Allí donde las voces se juntan nace un enorme cedro
Más confortable que el cielo

NATURAL FORCES

One glance
>to knock down the albatross

Two glances
>to stop the landscape
>at the river's edge

Three glances
>to change the girl into
>a kite

Four glances
>to hold back the train which
>falls in the chasm

Five glances
>to relight the stars
>blown out by the hurricane

Six glances
>to prevent the birth
>of the aquatic child

Seven glances
>to prolong the life of
>the bride

Eight glances
>to change the sea
>into sky

Nine glances
>to make the trees in the wood
>dance

Ten glances
>to see the beauty that is present
>between a dream and a catastrophe

[D.O. and C.H.]

LIFESCAPE

He leaves the end of the world to the accordion
Pays for the last song with rain
Out where the voices gather a giant cedar is born
More comfortable than the sky

Una golondrina me dice papá
Una anémona me dice mamá

Azul azul allí y en la boca del lobo
Azul Señor Cielo que se aleja
Qué dice usted Hacia dónde irá

Ah el hermoso brazo azul azul
Dad el brazo a la Señora Nube
Si tenéis miedo del lobo
El lobo de la boca azul azul
Del diente largo largo
Para devorar a la abuela naturaleza

Señor Cielo rasque su golondrina
Señora Nube apague sus anémonas

Las voces se juntan sobre el pájaro
Más grande que el árbol de la creación
Más hermoso que una corriente de aire entre dos astros

ELLA

Ella daba dos pasos hacia delante
Daba dos pasos hacia atrás
El primer paso decía buenos días señor
El segundo paso decía buenos días señora
Y los otros decían cómo está la familia
Hoy es un día hermoso como una paloma en el cielo

Ella llevaba una camisa ardiente
Ella tenía ojos de adormecedora de mares
Ella había escondido un sueño en un armario oscuro
Ella había encontrado un muerto en medio de su cabeza

Cuando ella llegaba dejaba una parte más hermosa muy lejos
Cuando ella se iba algo se formaba en el horizonte para esperarla
Sus miradas estaban heridas y sangraban sobre la colina
Tenía los senos abiertos y cantaba las tinieblas de su edad
Era hermosa como un cielo bajo una paloma

A swallow says papa to me
An anemone says mama to me

Blue blue there and in the mouth of the wolf
Blue Mr. Sky who goes off
What do you say Where will you go

Ah the beautiful blue blue arm
Give your arm to Mrs. Cloud
If you're afraid of the wolf
The wolf with the blue blue mouth
With the long long teeth
To eat up grandma nature

Mr. Sky scratch out your swallow
Mrs. Cloud put out your anemones

Above the bird the voices gather
Greater than the tree of creation
More beautiful than a flow of air between two stars   [D.M.G.]

SHE

She took two steps forward
She took two steps backward
The first step said good morning mister
The second step said good morning lady
And the other steps whispered how're the kids
This day's as lovely as a sky full of pigeons

She was wearing a burning brassiere
She had eyes rocked to sleep by the sea
She had buried her dreams in a windy closet
She had come on a dead man wedged in her head

When she got here one lovely part of her was still miles away
When she left something shot up on the skyline and waited for her
Her looks were bedsores and bled on the hill
When her breasts were opened she warbled the dusk of her age
She was lovely as the sky beneath a pigeon

Tenía una boca de acero
Y una bandera mortal dibujada entre los labios
Reía como el mar que siente carbones en su vientre
Como el mar cuando la luna se mira ahogarse
Como el mar que ha mordido todas las playas
El mar que desborda y cae en el vacío en los tiempos de abundancia
Cuando las estrellas arrullan sobre nuestras cabezas
Antes que el viento norte abra sus ojos
Era hermosa en sus horizontes de huesos
Con su camisa ardiente y sus miradas de árbol fatigado
Como el cielo a caballo sobre las palomas

CANCION DE MARCELO CIELOMAR

Mar cielo
Mar y cielo
Cielo y mar
El mar y el cielo
El cielo y el mar
El mar y su cielo
El cielo y su mar
El cielo y su madre
El mar y la madre
El mar y su padre
Mar y cielo y luna
Cielo de luna en el mar del cielo
Luna de mar en el cielo de luna
Mar de cielo en la luna de mar
El padre del mar en la madre del cielo de luna
Mar y cielo y luna y noche
La noche de la luna bajo el cielo de mar
El mar de noche sobre el cielo de la luna
La luna de cielo con la noche del mar
El cielo del mar con la noche de la luna
El padre de la luna de mar en la noche de la madre del cielo
El mar el cielo la luna la noche el viento
El viento
El mar al viento

She had a mouth made of steel
And the flag of death was scrawled on her lips
She laughed like the sea feeling coals in its belly
Like the sea with the moon drowning inside it
Like the sea when it's killed all its beaches
The sea that spills over that falls in the void when life gets too soft
When the stars gurgle over our heads
Before the North Wind has opened its eyes
She was lovely in her landscape of bones
With her burning brassiere and her look of a tree that's played out
Like the sky on horseback over the pigeons   [J.R.]

THE SONG OF MARCELO CIELOMAR

Sea sky
Sea and sky
Sky and sea
The sea and the sky
The sky and the sea
The sea and its sky
The sky and its sea
The sky and its mother
The sea and its mother
The sea and its father
Sea and sky and moon
Sky of moon in the sea of the sky
Moon of sea in the sky of moon
Sea of sky in the moon of sea
The father of the sea in the mother of the sky of moon
Sea and sky and moon and night
The night of the moon under the sky of sea
The sea of night over the sky of the moon
The moon of sky with the night of the sea
The sky of the sea with the night of the moon
The father of the moon of sea in the night of the mother of the sky
The sea the sky the moon the night the wind
The wind
The sea to the wind

El cielo al viento
La luna al viento
La noche al viento
El viento de mar
El viento de la luna
El cielo del viento
La noche del viento
El mar en el cielo sobre la noche de luna en el viento
El viento del cielo
El viento del cielo en la luna
El viento del cielo sobre el mar del viento
El viento del viento delante del viento
La noche de la luna al viento
El mar de la noche
El cielo de la luna
La noche de la luna en el mar del cielo al viento
La luna
El viento
El mar
El cielo
La noche
La luna de la luna llena
El viento del viento norte
El mar del altamar
El cielo del séptimo cielo
La noche de la noche eterna

LOS SEÑORES DE LA FAMILIA

Los ojos contra los ojos
El espacio contra el espacio
Señor qué hora es
No puedo contestarle
Soy el sobrino de la luna

The sky to the wind
The moon to the wind
The night to the wind
The wind of sea
The wind of the moon
The sky of the wind
The night of the wind
The sea in the sky over the night of moon in the wind
The wind of the sky
The wind of the sky in the moon
The wind of the sky over the sea of the wind
The wind of the wind before the wind
The night of the moon to the wind
The sea of the night
The sky of the moon
The night of the moon in the sea of the sky to the wind
The moon
The wind
The sea
The sky
The night
The moon of the full moon
The wind of the North Wind
The sea of the high seas
The sky of the seventh sky
The night of the eternal night   [D.O. and C.H.]

MEMBERS OF THE FAMILY

Eyes to eyes
Space to space
Sir what time is it
I can't tell you
I'm the moon's nephew

La nariz contra la nariz
La luna contra la luna
Señora qué día es hoy
Yo no puedo contestarle
Soy la hija del viento norte

La cabeza contra la cabeza
El viento contra el viento
Señor qué ciudad es ésta
Yo no puedo contestarle
Soy el padre del mar

La boca contra la boca
El mar contra el mar
Señora a dónde va este camino
Yo no puedo contestarle
Soy la prima del tiempo

La oreja contra la oreja
El tiempo contra el tiempo
Señor qué distancia tiene la vida
Yo no puedo contestarle
Soy el tío del cielo

Las voces contra las voces
La tierra contra la tierra
Los pies contra los pies
El cielo contra el cielo
La familia de los mudos tiene sangre de violín
Sale con el pie derecho a las calles de nuestros paisajes
Corta la naturaleza con un puñal
Y se aleja sobre un ojo que se pierde en el espacio

CANCION DE LA MUERVIDA

Mi mano derecha es una golondrina
Mi mano izquierda es un ciprés
Mi cabeza por delante es un señor vivo
Y por detrás es un señor muerto

Nose to nose
Moon to moon
Lady what day is it
I can't tell you
I'm the north wind's daughter

Head to head
Wind to wind
Sir what city is this
I can't tell you
I'm the sea's father

Mouth to mouth
Sea to sea
Lady where does this road go
I can't tell you
I'm time's cousin

Ear to ear
Time to time
Sir how long is life
I can't tell you
I'm the sky's uncle

Voices to voices
Earth to earth
Feet to feet
Sky to sky
The family of mutes has violin blood
Steps out on the streets of our landscapes right foot first
Cuts nature with a dagger
And goes off on an eye lost in space   [D.M.G.]

THE SONG OF THE DEATHLIFE

My right hand is a swallow
My left hand is a cypress
The front of my head is a living man
And the back is a dead man

Los muertos han perdido toda confianza
En los cimientos de nuestras casas y de nuestras lenguas
Y aun de nuestros relojes enrollados en el infinito
Qué podemos decirles
Ellos suben sobre el tejado de la eternidad
Y miran a lo lejos
Atan sólidamente las nubes que están llenas

Tocan la campana del vacío que debe saludar a los siglos
Como un sombrero
Llevan un anillo en cada uno de los cinco sentidos
Y un pájaro en cada cielo
Están desterrados de la tierra y encielados en el cielo
Ellos mondan la corteza de los siglos

Los vivos alargan su ciprés
Para decir buenos días a la golondrina
Se alejan sonrientes hasta el horizonte
Suben cantando hasta el piso de la muerte
Hablan con una lengua adormecida desde mucho tiempo
Son póstumos como los ecos de la flor del trueno
Y lo mismo que los perfumes
Llevan su cuerpo como el tallo de un nenúfar precioso
Y no van más lejos que un tiro de pistola
Cuentan los días con huesos de frutas
Que guardan en jaulas como pájaros
Cuentan las estrellas y les dan nombres amistosos y tibios
Es preciso no confundir los lechos y no equivocarse de plato
Es preciso cantar como un nenúfar precioso

Un pájaro trina para mil orejas anónimas
Una estrella brilla para mil ojos recién nacidos
El pájaro cambia de día con una mirada
La estrella deposita la muerte y sigue su camino

TENEMOS UN CATACLISMO ADENTRO

Los años suben como ramas a la punta
Suben al cielo y las montañas cruzan las manos a la muerte

The dead have lost all confidence
In the foundations of our houses and our tongues
And even in our watches wrapped up in the infinite
What could we tell them
They climb up over the roof of eternity
And look at the distance
They tie up tightly the clouds which are full

They ring the bell of emptiness which must salute the centuries
Like a hat
They carry a ring in each of the five senses
And a bird in each sky
They are exiled from earth and exhaled in the sky
They bite the rind of the centuries

The living extend their cypress
To say good morning to the swallow
They go away smiling towards the horizon
They climb up singing to the floor of death
They have spoken in a sleeping tongue for a long time
They are posthumous as the echoes of the thunder's flower
And the same as perfumes
They carry their body like the stem of a precious water lily
And do not go further than a pistol shot
They count days with the stones of fruit
Which they keep in cages like birds
They count the stars and give them warm and friendly names
One must not confuse the beds nor be mistaken about dishes
One must sing like a precious water lily

A bird trills for a thousand nameless ears
A star shines for a thousand newborn eyes
The bird changes the day with a glance
The star deposits death and goes on its way   [D.O. and C.H.]

THERE IS A CATACLYSM INSIDE US

The years burgeon at their tips like branches
They burgeon toward the sky and the mountains fold their hands in
    death

Entre campanadas de especie desconocida
Los entierros siguen a ciertos pájaros
En la noche de las flores sonámbulas
Y los brillos hipnóticos llenos de lágrimas

Por qué voy tras el viento de los sueños
Que agita mis cabellos rumorosos encima de la noche
Por las rutas solitarias como tristes palabras
No te pude encontrar
Ni siguiendo los rastros de una flor
Y sin embargo estás en algún sitio
Entre tu andar y la muerte
Con una alegría planetaria a flor de ojo

Nada recuerdo pero el sentimiento vive
Llevo en la carne los tiempos infantiles
Y los antes de los antes con sus ruidos confusos
Las épocas de los grandes principios
Y de las formaciones en fantasmagorías imprevisibles
Cuando el mar apenas aprendía a hablar
Y los árboles no sabían lo que iban a ser
Y la vida se estrellaba entre las rocas

Despiértame y grítame que estoy viviendo en hoy
Sé muy bien que si hubiera comido ciertas hierbas
Sería paloma mensajera
Y podría encontrarte a la sombra de esa flor que es la tarde
Pero el murmullo nada indica
Los barcos han partido hacia sus pájaros
Ya no es tiempo
Esto es lo único seguro entre los huracanes dados vuelta
Ya no es tiempo
La tarde se entierra seguida de sus selvas

Algo brilla en el aire
Sobre ese trozo de la tierra donde tú estás durmiendo
En donde las raíces ponen flores y otoños desgarradores
La vida se estrella en la cima de los montes
O no se estrella Para la noche es lo mismo

Todo es lo mismo para la noche
Y a veces para mí también

Between the sounding of uncharted bells
Funerals trail certain birds
In this night of sleepwalking flowers
             and the hypnotic spotlights full of tears

Why do I follow the wind through my dreams
As it stirs my murmuring hair on the roof of this night
Down deserted roads like sad words
I never could find you
Not even tracing the print of a flower
And yet I know you are somewhere
             between your footsteps and death
With the planetary joy of a flower emerging from each eye

I remember nothing but the feeling still lives
I bear my earliest days in my flesh
Day before the befores with their turbulent noises
The epochs of mighty beginnings
And formations into blind phantasmagorias
When the sea scarcely knew how to speak
And the trees couldn't tell what they would become
And life smashed itself on the rocks

Awaken me shout at me tell me I live in the present
I know damn well that if I'd eaten certain herbs
             I'd be a carrier pigeon
And I'd be able to find you in the shadow of that flower called evening
But the whispers don't tell me a thing
The ships have sailed off toward their birds
Time is all gone
This is the only sure thing in these cycles of hurricanes
Time is all gone
The evening buries itself alongside its forests

Something glows in the air
In that parcel of earth where you sleep
Where the roots hatch flowers and severing autumns
Life smashes itself on the summits of mountains
             or doesn't smash itself
                  But the night doesn't care

The night doesn't care about anything
And sometimes I don't care either

Ah ese cielo sereno con toda su eternidad
Y todo lo que se forma en sus entrañas
Y todo lo que palpita antes del amanecer
Ah la sed de infinito en relación a mi pecho
Desatad el árbol que tiene ansias de espacio
Recoged las velas de los astros cansados

Y tú anuncia la vida con tus ojos
Mira que el doble sueño no quiere terminar
Mira que el fantasma pudiera deshacerse
Y yo aún tengo palabras retenidas
Tengo cosas dolientes y cosas que susurran
Mira que las estrellas continuadas
Son como la voz que te canta y quiere ser interminable

Pero otros suben otros bajan
Ah cielo lleno de días y de noches
Amigos en dónde estáis amigos
Saliendo de palomas viene la muerte

RONDA DE LA VIDA RIENDO

I

Trescientos sesenta y cinco árboles tiene la selva
Trescientas sesenta y cinco selvas tiene el año
¿Cuántas se necesitan para formar un siglo?
Un niño se perdería en ellas hasta el fin del siglo
Y aprendería el canto de todos los pájaros

Los árboles doblan la cabeza cuando los niños lanzan piedras
Las piedras en el aire saludan a los pájaros y piden una canción
Una canción con los ojos azules
Una canción con los cabellos largos
Una canción dividida como una naranja
Con una historia adentro llena de sonrisas o si usted prefiere llena de
    lágrimas

Las lágrimas agitan las manos antes de ahogarse
Y las sonrisas saludan a las gentes desde lejos como las piedras

Ah that patient sky with all its eternity
And all that takes shape in its belly
And that throbs before daybreak
Ah the thirst for the infinite pressing my chest
Untie this tree that longs after space
Shorten the sails on those played-out stars

Proclaim life with your eyes
See how the double dream doesn't want to be over
How the phantoms could really be sloughed
And I still keep words in my throat
I keep painful things and things full of whispers
See how the stars that endure
            are like the voice that sings you
And wants to keep living forever

But others burgeon others decay
Ah sky full of days and of nights
Friends   where are you   friends
Scattering pigeons
            Here comes death   [J.R.]

SONG OF THE LAUGHING LIFE

I

The forest has three hundred and sixty-five trees
The year has three hundred and sixty-five forests
How many would you need to make a century?
A child would get lost in them till the end of the century
And would learn the song of every bird

Trees turn their heads as the children throw stones
In the air the stones greet the birds and ask for a song
A song with blue eyes
A song with long hair
A song split like an orange
With a story inside full of smiles or if you like full of tears
The tears wave their hands as they drown
And like the stones in the distance the smiles greet the people

Buenos días y Hasta luego son los hijos de la boca que va a enamorarse
   pronto
El sol también dice buenos días cuando los árboles aletean
Y dice hasta luego cuando la montaña cierra los ojos
Hasta luego entre las olas aceitadas del mar
Hasta luego diría yo también porque ahora el cielo trae una bandeja
   llena de flores
Así es agradable la vida como un jugo de naranja lleno de historias de
   niños entre los dientes de las niñas
Así es fresca la vida y puede correr como los perros entre los colores
   sueltos
O como los ríos que seguían a los abuelos

Las flores hacen gracias al borde del camino
Los árboles balbucean a nuestros ojos cosas tan claras que es imposible
   no comprender
Los árboles tienen quince años y las flores dan sus primeros pasos
Los árboles dicen buenos días y esperan que el sol se anude la corbata
   y se ponga el sombrero

Así es agradable la vida
La vida con su velocidad aterradora
La vida con trescientos sesenta y cinco árboles para escalar alegremente
La vida con sus flores como corbatas
La vida con sus mugidos trepando por la tarde
Lentos como los ojos de la tarde
El sol dice buenas noches y se va hasta que los árboles vuelvan a
   ocupar su sitio religiosamente

Así sería agradable la vida
Pero los hombres se miran con ojos de fogata
Se buscan en los rincones con dedos de puñales
Se buscan entre los árboles dormidos para hacerse esclavos
Entonces maldecimos la vida y empuñamos las manos
Entonces gritamos en las noches a la montaña
Viva la muerte con su velocidad aterradora
Con su velocidad que no enmohece nunca

II

Trescientos sesenta y cinco dedos tiene el árbol
Trescientas sesenta y cinco manos tienen los ojos azules

Good day and Good-bye are the mouth's children about to fall in love
The sun too says good day as the trees start to shake
And good-bye when the mountain shuts its eyes
Good-bye amid waves oiled by the sea
I'd say good-bye too because here comes the sky with a bowl full of
    flowers
So life is fine like an orange juice full of fairy tales between the teeth
    of little girls
So life is cool and can run like dogs amid bursting colors
Or like rivers that followed their ancestors

Flowers tell jokes by the side of the road
Trees murmur in our eyes things so clear it's impossible to misunder-
    stand
The trees are fifteen and the flowers just beginning to walk
The trees say good day and wait while the sun knots its tie and puts
    on its hat

So life is fine
Life with its terrifying speed
Life with its three hundred and sixty-five trees to go merrily climbing
Life with its flowers like neckties
Life with its moos rising in the afternoon
Slow like the eyes of the evening
The sun says good night and goes off till the trees religiously step back
    in their places

So life would be fine
But men look at each other with eyes full of fire
They search each other out in corners with fingers like daggers
They search among sleeping trees to make slaves of each other
Then we curse life and clench our fists
Then we scream at night to the mountain
Long live death with its terrifying speed
With its speed that never gets rusty

II

The tree has three hundred and sixty-five fingers
The blue eyes have three hundred and sixty-five hands

Lo mismo los ojos negros
Lo mismo los cabellos largos
Y las naranjas y las orejas que ruedan a través del siglo
Trescientos sesenta y cinco cantos tiene la garganta
Lo mismo las olas pedregosas del mar
Lo mismo las piedras aceitadas en el aire
Lo mismo la bandeja del cielo
Y el sol que dice buenas noches y cierra la puerta

Los bigotes del árbol encanecen rápidamente
Y se agitan al ritmo de su risa y de las risas de los niños
Los árboles tienen ochenta años y las risas dan los primeros pasos
Las lágrimas caen por el tronco del árbol
Las risas trepan por el cielo
Adentro del corazón se abre una naranja llena de luces y de colores
Los colores trepan por las ramas del árbol
Y trepan por los cabellos largos
Y se pasean al fondo de los ojos azules
O se pierden al fondo de los ojos negros

Buenos días y Hasta luego están parados al principio y al fin de cada
    historia
Y la historia está llena de árboles de niños de piedras y de olas
Los nietos dicen buenos días
Los abuelos dicen hasta luego
Los árboles crecen como los cabellos
Las olas brillan como los ojos azules
Los pájaros ríen como los ojos negros

Así es agradable la vida y puede cantar como las flores
Así es fresca la vida y puede reír como los ríos
La vida con su velocidad aterradora
La vida con sus árboles
Con sus sombreros
Con sus corbatas
Con sus ojos azules trepando por el cielo
Con sus cabellos largos cayendo por la tierra
La vida con el mugido de sus árboles en la tarde
La vida con sus piedras y sus olas enmohecidas
Con sus ríos que pasan mirando a todo el mundo
Con sus pájaros que aplauden las canciones

Same as black eyes
Same as long hair
And the oranges and the ears that spin through the century
The throat has three hundred and sixty-five songs
Same as the sea's pebbly waves
Same as the stones oiled in air
Same as the sky's bowl
And the sun that says good night and closes its door

The tree's mustaches grow rapidly gray
And sway to the rhythm of its laughter and the laughter of the children
The trees are eighty and the laughter just beginning to walk
Tears glide down the trunk of the tree
Laughter climbs through the sky
Inside the heart an orange full of lights and colors is opening
The colors climb through the branches of the tree
And climb on through long hair
And wander to the bottom of blue eyes
Or get lost in the depths of black eyes

Good day and Good-bye are standing at the beginning and the end of
    each story
And the story is filled with trees and with children with stones and
    with waves
The grandchildren say good day
The grandparents say good-bye
The trees grow like hair
The waves shine like blue eyes
The birds laugh like black eyes

So life is fine and can sing like the flowers
So life is cool and can laugh like the rivers
Life with its terrifying speed
Life with its trees
With its hats
With its neckties
With its blue eyes climbing through the sky
With its long hair falling through the earth
Life with the cry of its trees in the evening
Life with its stones and its rusty waves
With its rivers that flow by staring at everyone
With its birds that applaud the songs

Así sería agradable la vida
Pero hay aún muchos fantasmas que se pasean por la vida
Fabricantes de mártires para cubrir el canto de las olas espiando que la
    presa se distraiga
Ellos se pasean con las manos en los bolsillos
Con la arrogancia en el hueco del sombrero
Y un látigo en cada ojo
Se pasean en sus zapatos luminosos como ataúdes
Se pasean como ataúdes en sus ataúdes

Esos espectros viven de la sangre de millones de hombres
Y porque ellos viven en la vida la vida es detestable
Y los hombres prefieren la muerte
La muerte con su marcha que no enmohece nunca

III

Trescientos sesenta y cinco pájaros tiene el cielo
Estos pájaros serán banderas el día del gran triunfo
Cuando los hombres oigan cantar la hora del hombre
Cuando nadie viva del esfuerzo nacido en otros pechos
Cuando nadie se nutra de la carne ajena
Ni respire por pulmones extraños
Ni se ate los pantalones con las tripas esclavas

Trescientos sesenta y cinco paisajes tiene el ojo
Estos paisajes cantarán solos el día del gran triunfo
Cantarán con la alegría de sus árboles tremolantes
Porque cayeron las cabezas de todos los espectros
Porque ya desangraron todos los fantasmas
Y se cerraron los ojos que tenían látigos
Y las bocas antropófagas de dientes arrogantes

Ahora se puede cantar
Millones de hombres pueden cantar
Un canto inmenso como una montaña que trepa por el cielo
Se soltaron las canciones amarradas
Y el viento les dio la dirección de su esperanza

Trescientas sesenta y cinco canciones suben al espacio
Canciones con los ojos azules
Canciones con los ojos negros

So life would be fine
But there are still many phantoms wandering through life
Makers of martyrs to cloak the song of the waves waiting till the prey
    is distracted
They pass with their hands in their pockets
With arrogance in the crease of their hats
And a whip in each eye
They pass in shoes shined like caskets
They pass like caskets inside caskets

Those specters live off the blood of millions of men
And because they live in life life is hateful
And men prefer death
Death with its step that never gets rusty

III

The sky has three hundred and sixty-five birds
These birds will be flags the day of the great triumph
When men hear man's hour sung
When no one lives off the strength born in another's breast
When no one feeds on another's flesh
Nor breathes through a stranger's lungs
Nor ties his pants with slave gut

The eye has three hundred and sixty-five landscapes
Each landscape will sing a solo the day of the great triumph
They will sing with the joy of their waving trees
Because the heads of all the specters have fallen
Because all the phantoms have bled to death
And the eyes that held whips
And the man-eating mouths with arrogant teeth have been closed

Now we can sing
Millions of men can sing
A song great as a mountain that climbs through the sky
The bound songs have been freed
And the wind shows them the course of their hope

Three hundred and sixty-five songs leap into space
Songs with blue eyes
Songs with black eyes

Canciones con árboles gigantescos
Canciones con olas infatigables

Los dientes de los hombres ríen como los dientes de los niños
Cuando hablan en secreto a las niñas
El sol sale con traje nuevo a su trabajo diario
Los árboles suben hasta su propia punta sin descanso
Las olas chillan y se dan vueltas de carnero
Y los niños cantan
El sol cabizbajo
Sonando el badajo
Salió esta mañana
Muy tieso y muy majo
Con el cielo a cuestas
Y una nube al fajo

Murió el fantasma que se nutría de pulmones
Las canciones sueltan sus amarras por los mares libres
Murió el vampiro que sorbía los globos de la luz
Las flores lanzan campanadas sobre el mundo
Murieron las aves de rapiña en su leyenda negra
Las olas juegan como los niños
Murió el señor de las batallas y la señora de las llagas
Los árboles bailan tomados de la mano
El viento nuevo borró todas las fronteras
Las fronteras dijeron adiós y dieron el último suspiro
La tierra las enterró bajo la tierra

Así es agradable la vida
Y la vida aplaude a la vida
Las sonrisas aplauden al viento
Las canciones aplauden a los pájaros
Los pájaros aplauden a la luz
La luz aplaude a los árboles
Los árboles aplauden al cielo
El cielo aplaude al sol
El sol aplaude a las olas

Y toda la vida es un teatro de aplausos
Así es agradable la vida y puede bailar como las flores
Que sueltan sus colores y sus perfumes de alegría

Songs with great trees
Songs with tireless waves

Men's teeth laugh like children's teeth
As they whisper secrets to young girls
The sun comes out in new clothes for its daily work
Trees race to their tops without stopping
Waves shriek and do somersaults
And children sing
The sun deep in thought
Sounding its bell
Came out this morning
Very proper and elegant
With the sky on its back
And a cloud in its bundle

Dead the phantom that fed on lungs
Songs slip their moorings for open seas
Dead the vampire that sucked on globes of light
Flowers spread bell tolls over the world
Dead the birds of prey in their black habit
Waves play like children
Dead the lord of battles and the lady of wounds
Trees join hands and dance
The new wind erased all the borders
The borders said farewell and gave their last sigh
The land buried them under the earth

So life is fine
And life applauds life
Smiles applaud the wind
Songs applaud the birds
Birds applaud the light
Light applauds the trees
Trees applaud the sky
The sky applauds the sun
The sun applauds the waves

And all of life is a theater of applause
So life is fine and can dance like the flowers
Which set free their colors and their perfumes of joy   [D.M.G.]

PESOS Y MEDIDAS

Las mágicas gallinas en su planeta alegre
Fabrican huevos sobre medida
Como los árboles encomendados a la tierra
Con precisión se mide el río de estrella en estrella
La luna mide el cielo lentamente
Y nadie ha oído nunca el ruido de sus pasos
La campana fabrica campanadas tan exactas
Que no hay sorpresa o muy pequeño margen
Como un alma conocida en todas sus sombras
En sus rumores y sus incitaciones al fuego
A las lejanías y al cerca de su tallo

Los astros conocen sus kilómetros
Las ramas su potencia futura
La piedra su caída preparada en la primera noche de los tiempos
La lluvia es a medida de su nube
Y su velocidad se ajusta al peso y la atracción
Como el choque de dos bocas que se aman

Sobre medida ladran los perros
Porque el fantasma se rasca la cabeza
Sobre medida canta el canario
Porque tiene medidos los veranos
Sobre medida corre la Tierra
Como una bala al corazón del éter distraído

SIN POR QUE

Arum arum
Por qué he dicho arum
Por qué ha venido a mí sin timonel
Y al azar de los vientos
Qué significa esta palabra sin ojos
Ni manos de estrella
Tú la has puesto en mi cabeza
Es la noche que la trajo a mis oídos
La noche de mi oído abierto a los peligros

WEIGHTS AND MEASURES

The magic hens in their happy planet
Make eggs to measure
Like trees committed to earth
Precisely the river measures itself from star to star
The moon measures the sky slowly
And no one has ever heard the sound of its steps
The bell rings out very exactly
So there is no surprise or very little margin
Like a soul known in all its shadows
In its noises and its invocations to fire
To the distances and close to its stem

The stars know their mileages
The branches their future strength
The stone its fall prepared in the first night of time
The rain is made to the measure of its cloud
And it adjusts its speed to the weight and attraction
Like the clash of two mouths which are in love

The dogs bark to measure
Because the phantom scratches its head
The canary sings to measure
Because it has the measure of summers
Time runs to measure
Like a bullet to the heart of the heedless ether

[D.O. and C.H.]

WITHOUT REASON

Humm humm
Why have I said humm
Why has it come to me without a helmsman
And at the whim of the winds
What does this word mean without eyes
Or a star's hands
You have put it into my head
It is the night that brought it to my ears
The night of my ears open to dangers

Después de un largo camino de bosques en marcha
Y el sueño preparado
El sueño pronto
Pronto prontooo

Arum arum
Arum en mi cerebro
Arum en mis miradas
Toda mi cabeza es arum
Mis manos son arum
El mundo es arum
Arum el infinito
Arum me cierra el paso
Es un muro enorme ante mis pies

Arum del sufrimiento girando en su molino
Arum de la alegría
De mi fatiga y de mis vértigos
Quiero morir
He naufragado al fondo de mi alma
En algo repentino y sin raíces
Arum me mata
Dulce asesino tan gratuito
Como el canario de alta mar
Arum arum

FIN DE CUENTAS

Ha llegado el ja ja con su fin de canción en llamas
Con su estrella de dolor
Y su dolor de cabeza
Y su cabeza de más lejos
Y su más lejos de fiebre rumorosa
Ha llegado y se ha ido
Con los pies de visita y dolor disfrazado
Con la gracia de su cornisa
Ha llegado y se ha ido
Por la colina de sus muertos ávidos de pena

After a long road of marching forests
And prepared sleep
Sleep soon
Soon soooon

Humm humm
Humm in my brain
Humm in my glances
My whole head is humm
My hands are humm
The world is humm
Humm the infinite
Humm closes off my path
It is an enormous wall in front of my feet

Humm of suffering turning in its mill
Humm of happiness
Of my fatigue and my dizziness
I want to die
I've shipwrecked at the depths of my soul
On something sudden and rootless
Humm kills me
Sweet murderer so gratuitous
Like the canary of the high seas
Humm humm   [D.O. and C.H.]

END OF THE STORY

The ha-ha has come with its song's end in flames
With its star of pain
And its head of pain
And its head of distance
And its distance of murmuring fever
It has come and gone
With its feet of visiting and pain in disguise
With the grace of its cornice
It has come and gone
To the hill of its dead men eager for sorrow

Ha llegado el oh oh con sus luces de cascada
Con sus pájaros sin origen estudiado
Con su sueños de árbol frente al clima
Y su árbol de tímpano
Y su tímpano de linterna venenosa
Como las bellas brujas de antaño
Que se fueron y volverán sobre las olas
A sacar de las tumbas la materia prima
A cantar en torrentes de lava
Y llenar de mariposas los vestidos de las madres
Que no pueden olvidar la voz lejana
Que no pueden recordar el perfume perdido

Ha llegado el ja ja
Para hacer optimistas las lámparas cansadas
Y dar color al aire y dar campo a los labios
Ha llegado el oh oh
Para que lo admiremos
En su redoma de chispas nadadoras

ANUNCIO

La sonrisa en el rincón de los labios
Donde mueren las sonrisas
En la noche cuando las piedras lloran
Lágrimas muy amargas

Alguien sabrá el futuro y su paisaje de astros
Las palabras que llenan el dolor de horizontes de luto

Entra el astrólogo vestido de poemas
Como las nubes de arroyos
Habla y anda como la noche
En la cumbre de sus frases un pájaro se muere

Nada importa
Amor y enigma mantenido
El es de otra opinión
Porque sólo cree en los fósforos de la inconsciencia

The oh-oh has come with its lights of a waterfall
With its birds without studied origin
With its dreams of a tree facing the weather
And its eardrum tree
And its eardrum of poisonous lantern
Like the beautiful witches of long ago
Who left and returned over the waves
To dig raw material out of graves
To sing in torrents of lava
To fill the mothers' dresses with butterflies
They cannot forget the far-off voice
They cannot remember the lost perfume

The ha-ha has come
To make optimists of the tired lamps
And give color to air and give space to lips
The oh-oh has come
So we can admire it
In its flask of swimming embers   [D.O. and C.H.]

ANNOUNCEMENT

The smile in the corner of the lips
Where smiles die
At night when the stones weep
Such bitter tears

Someone must know the future and its landscape of stars
The words which fill the sadness with horizons of grief

The astrologer enters dressed in poems
Like river clouds
He speaks and he moves like the night
On the summit of his words a bird is dying

Nothing matters
Love and enigma continue
He is of another opinion
Because he believes only in the stars of the unconscious

En la espada de la soledad
Que corta en dos nuestro silencio
Para que sea diálogo de aire y nada

Oh noche crucificada sobre el viento
Oh noche
Buenas noches

In the blade of solitude
Which cuts our silence in two
So that air and nothingness might converse

Oh night crucified upon the wind
Oh night
Good night

El Ciudadano del Olvido

The Citizen of Oblivion

1941

RINCONES SORDOS

El mundo se detiene a medio camino
Con su cielo prendido en las montañas
Y el alba en ciertas flores que yo conozco

Esconde en tus cabellos los secretos de la noche
Esconde las mentiras en tu alma de alegres sombras
Esconde tus alas bajo tus besos
Esconde el collar de suspiros en torno a tus senos
Esconde la barca de tu lengua en las fuentes de la sed
En el puerto de la boca amarrada
Esconde la luz a la sombra
Las lágrimas al abrigo del viento que va a soplar
Porque tiene derecho a la vida
Como yo lo tengo a la más alta cumbre
Y al abismo que ha caído tan bajo

Esconde las caídas del sueño
Esconde los colores al fondo de los ojos
Esconde el mar detrás del cielo
Y vuelve a subir a la superficie
Para ser tú mismo al sol de los destinos
A flor de mano como el ciego olvidado

Esconde los suspiros en su estuche
Esconde las palabras en su fruto
Y llora tu vida en el hastío de las cosas

SOLO

Solo solo entre la noche y la muerte
Andando en medio de la eternidad
Comiendo una fruta en medio del vacío

La noche La muerte
El muerto recién plantado en el infinito
La tierra se va la tierra vuelve

Solo con una estrella al frente
Solo con un gran canto adentro y ninguna estrella al frente

QUIET SPACES

The world stops in the middle of its course
Its sky caught on mountains
And the sunrise on certain flowers I recognize

It hides the secrets of the night in your hair
It hides lies in your soul of bright shadows
It hides your wings beneath your kisses
It hides the necklace of sighs around your breasts
It hides the barge of your tongue in its fountains of thirst
In the harbor of the fastened mouth
It hides the light from the darkness
The tears in the shelter of the wind soon to burst
Because it has a right to life
Just as I have it from the highest peak
To the abyss which has fallen so low

It hides dreams' failures
It hides colors at the bottom of eyes
It hides the sea behind the sky
And comes back up to the surface
To be yourself beneath the sun of destiny
Like the soft touch of the forgotten blind man

It hides sighs in its case
It hides words in its fruit
And your life weeps for the boredom of it all   [D.M.G.]

ALONE

Alone between night and death alone
Travelling through the heart of eternity
Eating fruit at the center of the void

Night Death
The dead just planted in the infinite
The earth leaves the earth returns

Alone with a star before me
Alone with a great song inside and no star before me

La noche y la muerte
La noche de la muerte
La muerte de la noche rondando por la muerte

Tan lejos tan lejos
El mundo se va por el viento
Y un perro aúlla de infinito buscando la tierra perdida

TIEMPO DE ESPERA

Pasan los días
La eternidad no llega ni el milagro

Pasan los días
El barco no se acerca
El mar no se hace flor ni campanario
No se descubre la caída

Pasan los días
Las piedras lloran con sus huesos azules
Pero no se abre la puerta
No se descubre la caída de la noche
Ni la ciencia en su cristal
Ni el comprender ni la apariencia ni la hojarasca del porqué
Pasan los días
No sale adolescencia
Ni atmósfera vivida ni misterio

Pasan los días
El ojo no se hace mundo
Las tristezas no se hacen pensamiento
El mar no llega hasta mis pies agonizando

Pasan los días
Y ella es pulmón de noches rompiéndose en sonidos
Y es hermosa como llanura comprendida
Es abundancia de sauces y silencios

Pasan los días
Ella es huracán que desata sus ruidos

Night and death
Death's night
Night's death spinning through death

So far far away
The world flies off in the wind
And a dog howls in the infinite searching for the lost land

[D.M.G.]

TIME OF WAITING

The days pass
Neither eternity nor the miracle arrive

The days pass
The ship doesn't come
The sea doesn't turn into a flower or a belfry
The fall is not uncovered

The days pass
The stones weep with their blue bones
But the door doesn't open
The fall of night is not revealed
Nor science in its crystal
Nor understanding nor the appearance or the leafstorm of whys
The days pass
Youth doesn't come
Nor living air nor the mystery

The days pass
The eye doesn't turn into the world
Sorrows don't become thought
The sea doesn't come dying at my feet

The days pass
And she is the lung of the night breaking into music
And she is as beautiful as an open field
Full of willows and silences

The days pass
She is a hurricane unleashing her noises

Es una gran lágrima cayendo interminablemente
Como una estrella que se volviera loca

Pasan los días
El miraje infinito de las tumbas una a una
No detiene la marcha
Se abren paso hacia el día hacia las horas
Hacia la edad y sus malezas

Pasan los días
Y no se oye el ruido de la luna

LA VIDA AL AIRE

Corriendo en arena alegre hasta el fin del pensamiento
Buscando a tientas los trozos perdidos y las hojas de nostalgias armoniosas
La más hermosa sabe que ha de llegar un día grande como las edades

El corazón estruja el agua de su esponja
Y corre por las noches de su vida
Vestido de sangre y desnudando al tiempo
Entre su arena lenta y su ataúd

El corazón sabe que hay un mañana atado
Y que hay que libertar
Y vive en sus silencios y su luz desgraciada
Como el brillo que los faroles han robado a los árboles

UN DIA VENDRA

Una mirada perdida en el pájaro
Un pájaro perdido en la mirada
Una ciudad secreta en el pecho de una mujer
Viaja a pie descalzo a través de los vientos favorables

Las olas perseguidas por los ojos
Las olas perseguidas por el silencio

She is a great tear endlessly falling
Like a star going mad

The days pass
The infinite mirage of tombs
Never slowing its pace
Gently open one by one on the day and the hours
On the age and all its weeds

The days pass
And the sound of the moon is not heard   [D.M.G.]

LIFE IN THE AIR

Running in sand happy till the end of thought
Groping in the dark for lost fragments and the leaves of harmonious
    nostalgias
The most beautiful woman knows that a day as great as the ages has
    arrived

The heart squeezes the water from its sponge
And runs through the nights of its life
Dressed in blood and undressing time
Between its slow sand and its coffin

The heart knows there is a captive morning
And that it must be freed
And it lives in its silences and its sad light
Like the glow the lamp posts have stolen from the trees   [D.M.G.]

A DAY WILL COME

A glance lost in the bird
A bird lost in the glance
A secret city in the breast of a woman
Travelling barefoot across favorable winds
Waves pursued by eyes
Waves pursued by silence

El silencio en la mirada del pájaro
Las olas en la mirada del silencio
El pájaro en la mirada de las olas
Y las miradas del pájaro en las olas

Vuestro fantasma es un campo cerrado como una garganta
Como una lágrima de silencio en los ojos del pájaro
¿En dónde está el desierto recordando su infancia
Y la mano sin sombra sedienta de sorpresas?
Queremos el camino del trueno
Y un pensamiento desgarrador en lugar de una estrella

Es preciso crear la luz y el sueño
En el hueco de la mano
Es preciso extender el desierto de la sombra hasta las orillas del huracán
Transportar el mar a la montaña
Descubrir una lágrima como un continente
El pájaro perseguido por las olas es favorable

El desierto está ávido de sorpresas y del fantasma sin reflejos
Esto hace a la sombra bajar de la montaña
Esto hace cerrar las rejas del océano
Y que la lluvia caiga sobre las mirades del viento

Fantasma en libertad sobre los puentes
Sobre los puentes del pecho y la cabeza
De pecho peligroso a pecho frío
De cabeza en cabeza
Con sus mercaderías de sueños y de anuncios

Fantasma en libertad sobre los mares
Canta el triunfo del que trabaja sobre aquel que paga
Canta la muerte del que fabrica esclavos en yunques dolorosos
Canta la bandera del alba que marcha
Roja como los ojos de la cólera y sus mareas
Como los ojos que han llorado largos siglos

Canta fantasma
Una ciudad perdida en el pájaro
Un pájaro perdido en el pecho de una mujer
Un viento perdido en la ciudad
Canta fantasma en libertad sobre los árboles
Un viento perdido en la mirada de un pájaro
Un mundo naciente que se eleva del mar en silencio
Un mundo mecido en los brazos de las olas

Silence in the glance of the bird
Waves in the glance of silence
The bird in the glance of waves
And in the waves glances of the bird

Your vision is a field shut like a throat
Like a silent tear in the eye of the bird
Where's the desert recalling its childhood
And the shadowless hand thirsting for surprises?
We seek the road of thunder
And blistering thought in place of a star

We have to create light and dreams
In the palm of the hand
We have to spread the shadow's desert to the banks of the hurricane
To bring the sea to the mountain
To discover a tear like a continent
The bird pursued by waves is favorable

The desert is hungry for surprises and for the unreflected vision
This makes the shadow come down from the mountain
This makes the gates of the ocean close
And the rain fall on the glances of the wind

Visions of freedom over the bridges
Over bridges of breasts and heads
From dangerous breast to cool breast
From head to head
With their goods of dreams and news

Visions of freedom over the seas
Singing the triumph of the one who works over the one who pays
Singing the death of the one who makes slaves on pitiless anvils
Singing the dawn's flag that goes out
Red as the eyes of rage and their shores
Like eyes that have wept long centuries

Visions sing
A city lost in the bird
A bird lost in the breast of a woman
A wind lost in the city
Visions of freedom sing above the trees
A wind lost in the glance of a bird
A world growing rising from the sea in silence
A world rocked in the arms of the waves   [D.M.G.]

Ultimos Poemas

Last Poems

1948

AIRE DE ALBA

Mi alma está sobre el mar y silba un sueño
Decid a los pastores que el viento prepara su caballo
Y saluda al partir en el orgullo de su infancia
Yo amo una mujer de orgullo y sueño
Desembarcando de su fondo silenciosa
Sabed pastores que debéis cuidarme
Y cuidar sus sueños y cuidar sus cantos
Y la fiesta de las olas
Como alegría de su orgullo y su belleza

Ah cielo azul para la reina al viento
Ah rebaño de cabras y cabellos blancos
Labios de elogios y cabellos rubios
Animales perdidos en sus ojos
Hablad a la osamenta que se peina
En el país del fondo hasta el fin de los siglos
Túnica y cetro
Amplificación de los recuerdos
Ruido de insectos y caminos
Hablad de la comarca como corre el océano
Ah el viento
El viento se detiene para la reina que sale de su cielo

LA VIDA ES SUEÑO

Los ojos andan de día en día
Las princesas pasan de rama en rama
Como la sangre de los enanos
Que cae igual que todas sobre las hojas
Cuando llega su hora de noche en noche

Las hojas muertas quieren hablar
Son gemelas de su voz dolorida
Son la sangre de las princesas
Y los ojos de rama en rama
Que caen igual que los astros viejos
Con las alas rotas como corbatas

DAWN AIR

My soul's above the sea and whistling a dream
Tell the shepherds the wind is saddling its horse
And waving as it leaves in the pride of its youth
I love a woman proud and dreamlike
Silent stepping out from her center
Shepherds know that you should watch me
And watch your dreams and watch your songs
And the dance of the waves
Like the joy of their pride and beauty

Ah sky blue for the queen in the wind
Ah herd of goats and white hair
Lips of praise and red hair
Animals lost in her eyes
Speak to the skeleton combing its hair
From the tip of the earth to the end of the ages
Tunic and scepter
Amplification of memories
Sound of insects and highways
Speak of the land as the ocean flows
Ah the wind
The wind stops for the queen who steps out from her sky

[D.M.G.]

LA VIDA ES SUEÑO

The eyes pass from day to day
Princesses climb from branch to branch
Like the blood of dwarves
Which falls like everyone's upon the leaves
When the time comes night after night

The dead leaves want to speak
They are twins with their sad voice
They are the blood of princesses
And the eyes from branch to branch
Which fall like old stars
With wings revolving like neckties

La sangre cae de rama en rama
De ojo en ojo y de voz en voz
La sangre cae como las corbatas
No puede huir saltando como los enanos
Cuando las princesas pasan
Hacia sus astros doloridos
Como las alas de las hojas
Como los ojos de las olas
Como las hojas de los ojos
Como las olas de las alas

Las horas caen de minuto en minuto
Como la sangre
Que quiere hablar

LA POESIA ES UN ATENTADO CELESTE

Yo estoy ausente pero en el fondo de esta ausencia
Hay la espera de mí mismo
Y esta espera es otro modo de presencia
La espera de mi retorno
Yo estoy en otros objetos
Ando en viaje dando un poco de mi vida
A ciertos árboles y a ciertas piedras
Que me han esperado muchos años

Se cansaron de esperarme y se sentaron

Yo no estoy y estoy
Estoy ausente y estoy presente en estado de espera
Ellos querrían mi lenguaje para expresarse
Y yo querría el de ellos para expresarlos
He aquí el equívoco el atroz equívoco

Angustioso lamentable
Me voy adentrando en estas plantas
Voy dejando mis ropas
Se me van cayendo las carnes
Y mi esqueleto se va revistiendo de cortezas

The blood falls from branch to branch
From eye to eye and from voice to voice
The blood falls like neckties
It can't stop jumping like dwarves
As the princesses climb
Toward their sad stars
Like the wings of leaves
Like the eyes of waves
Like the leaves of eyes
Like the waves of wings

The hours fall from minute to minute
Like blood
That wants to speak   [D.M.G.]

POETRY IS A HEAVENLY CRIME

I am absent but deep in this absence
There is the waiting for myself
And this waiting is another form of presence
The waiting for my return
I am in other objects
I am away travelling giving a little of my life
To some trees and some stones
That have been waiting for me many years

They got tired of waiting for me and sat down

I'm not here and I'm here
I'm absent and I'm present in a state of waiting
They wanted my language so they could express themselves
And I wanted theirs to express them
This is the ambiguity, the horrible ambiguity

Tormented wretched
I'm moving inward on these soles
I'm leaving my clothes behind
My flesh is falling away on all sides
And my skeleton's putting on bark

Me estoy haciendo árbol Cuántas veces me he ido convirtiendo en otras
    cosas . . .
Es doloroso y lleno de ternura

Podría dar un grito pero se espantaría la transubstanciación
Hay que guardar silencio Esperar en silencio

MONUMENTO AL MAR

Paz sobre la constelación cantante de las aguas
Entrechocadas como los hombros de la multitud
Paz en el mar a las olas de buena voluntad
Paz sobre la lápida de los naufragios
Paz sobre los tambores del orgullo y las pupilas tenebrosas
Y si yo soy el traductor de las olas
Paz también sobre mí

He aquí el molde lleno de trizaduras del destino
El molde de la venganza
Con sus frases iracundas despegándose de los labios
He aquí el molde lleno de gracia
Cuando eres dulce y estás allí hipnotizado por las estrellas
He aquí la muerte inagotable desde el principio del mundo
Porque un día nadie se paseará por el tiempo
Nadie a lo largo del tiempo empedrado de planetas difuntos

Este es el mar
El mar con sus olas propias
Con sus propios sentidos
El mar tratando de romper sus cadenas
Queriendo imitar la eternidad
Queriendo ser pulmón o neblina de pájaros en pena
O el jardín de los astros que pesan en el cielo
Sobre las tinieblas que arrastramos
O que acaso nos arrastran
Cuando vuelan de repente todas las palomas de la luna
Y se hace más obscuro que las encrucijadas de la muerte

El mar entra en la carroza de la noche
Y se aleja hacia el misterio de sus parajes profundos

I'm turning into a tree How often I've turned into other things . . .
It's painful and full of tenderness

I could cry out but it would scare away the transubstantiation
Must keep silence Wait in silence   [W.S.M.]

MONUMENT TO THE SEA

Peace above the singing constellation of waters
Crashing like the shoulders of the masses
Peace in the sea to the waves of good will
Peace above the tombstones of the shipwrecked
Peace above the drums of pride and the dark pupils of the eye
And if I'm the translator of waves
Peace too above me

Here's the cast filled with bits of destiny
The cast of vengeance
With bitter words flying from its lips
Here's the cast full of grace
When you're calm standing there hypnotized by the stars
Here's death unexhausted since the beginning of the world
Because one day no one will walk through time
No one through time lined with dead planets

This is the sea
The sea with its own waves
With its own meanings
The sea trying to break its chains
Wanting to be eternity
Wanting to be lung or mist of birds in mourning
Or the garden of stars hanging in the sky
Above the shadows we're dragging
Or which perhaps are dragging us
When suddenly all the moon's doves fly off
And it's darker than the crossroads of death

The sea gets in the night's coach
And heads off for the mystery of its deepest points

Se oye apenas el ruido de las ruedas
Y el ala de los astros que penan en el cielo
Este es el mar
Saludando allá lejos la eternidad
Saludando a los astros olvidados
Y a las estrellas conocidas

Este es el mar que se despierta como el llanto de un niño
El mar abriendo los ojos y buscando el sol con sus pequeñas manos tem-
    blorosas
El mar empujando las olas
Sus olas que barajan los destinos

Levántate y saluda el amor de los hombres,

Escucha nuestras risas y también nuestro llanto
Escucha los pasos de millones de esclavos
Escucha la protesta interminable
De esa angustia que se llama hombre
Escucha el dolor milenario de los pechos de carne
Y la esperanza que renace de sus propias cenizas cada día

También nosotros te escuchamos
Rumiando tantos astros atrapados en tus redes
Rumiando eternamente los siglos naufragados
También nosotros te escuchamos
Cuando te revuelcas en tu lecho de dolor
Cuando tus gladiadores se baten entre sí
Cuando tu cólera hace estallar los meridianos
O bien cuando te agitas como un gran mercado en fiesta
O bien cuando maldices a los hombres
O te haces el dormido
Tembloroso en tu gran telaraña esperando la presa

Lloras sin saber por qué lloras
Y nosotros lloramos creyendo saber por qué lloramos
Sufres sufres como sufren los hombres
Que oiga rechinar tus dientes en la noche
Y te revuelques en tu lecho
Que el insomnio no te deje calmar tus sufrimientos
Que los niños apedreen tus ventanas
Que te arranquen el pelo

You can hardly hear the sound of its wheels
And the beating of stars weeping in the sky
This is the sea
Greeting eternity way off
Greeting the forgotten stars
And the known stars

This is the sea that wakes up like the cry of a child
The sea opening its eyes and looking for the sun with its small hands
    trembling
The sea pushing its waves
The waves shuffling destinies

Get up and welcome man's love

Listen to our cries and our laughter
Listen to the steps of millions of slaves
Listen to the endless protest
Of that anguish known as man
Listen to that ancient scream from the breasts of flesh
And to the hope that's reborn from their own ashes every day

We hear you too
Contemplating all those stars trapped in your nets
Eternally contemplating the shipwrecked centuries
We hear you too
When you turn over in your bed of sorrow
When your gladiators fight among themselves
When your anger makes the meridians explode
Or when you shake like a great market at festival
Or even when you curse men
Or pretend to be asleep
Trembling in your giant web waiting for the catch

You weep without knowing why you weep
And we weep thinking we know why we weep
You suffer you suffer like men suffer
May your teeth chatter through the night
And may you toss in your bed
May insomnia never let your sufferings cease
May children throw stones at your windows
May they pull out your hair

Tose tose revienta en sangre tus pulmones
Que tus resortes enmohezcan
Y te veas pisoteado como césped de tumba

Pero soy vagabundo y tengo miedo que me oigas
Tengo miedo de tus venganzas
Olvida mis maldiciones y cantemos juntos esta noche
Hazte hombre te digo como yo a veces me hago mar
Olvida los presagios funestos
Olvida la explosión de mis praderas
Yo te tiendo las manos como flores
Hagamos las paces te digo
Tú eres el más poderoso
Que yo estreche tus manos en las mías
Y sea la paz entre nosotros

Junto a mi corazón te siento
Cuando oigo el gemir de tus violines
Cuando estás ahí tendido como el llanto de un niño
Cuando estás pensativo frente al cielo
Cuando estás dolorido en tus almohadas
Cuando te siento llorar detrás de mi ventana
Cuando lloramos sin razón como tú lloras

He aquí el mar
El mar donde viene a estrellarse el olor de las ciudades
Con su regazo lleno de barcas y peces y otras cosas alegres
Esas barcas que pescan a la orilla del cielo
Esos peces que escuchan cada rayo de luz
Esas algas con sueños seculares
Y esa ola que canta mejor que las otras

He aquí el mar
El mar que se estira y se aferra a sus orillas
El mar que envuelve las estrellas en sus olas
El mar con su piel martirizada
Y los sobresaltos de sus venas
Con sus días de paz y sus noches de histeria

Y al otro lado qué hay al otro lado
Qué escondes mar al otro lado
El comienzo de la vida largo como una serpiente

Cough cough until your lungs explode in blood
May your springs grow rusty
And may you see yourself trampled on like the grass around a grave

But I'm a wanderer and I'm afraid you might hear me
I'm afraid of your vengeance
Forget my curses and let's sing together tonight
I say make yourself a man like I sometimes make myself sea
Forget the sad omens
Forget the outburst of my prairies
I stretch my hands to you like flowers
I say let's make peace
You're the greater force
Let me squeeze your hands in mine
And let peace exist between us

I feel you by my heart
When I hear the hum of your violins
When you're there stretched out like the tears of a child
When you're deep in thought in front of the sky
When I hear you weeping behind my window
When for no reason we weep as you weep

Here's the sea
The sea where the stench of the cities comes to shatter
With its lap full of ships and fish and other joyous things
Those ships fishing at the shore of the sky
Those fish listening to each ray of light
That seaweed with its ageless dreams
And that wave singing better than the rest

Here's the sea
The sea expanding and anchoring itself
The sea wrapping stars in its waves
The sea with its martyred skin
And the shocks of its veins
With its days of peace and its nights of hysteria

And on the other side what's happening on the other side
Sea what are you hiding on the other side
The beginning of life as long as a snake

O el comienzo de la muerte más honda que tú mismo
Y más alta que todos los montes
Qué hay al otro lado
La milenaria voluntad de hacer una forma y un ritmo
O el torbellino eterno de pétalos tronchados

He ahí el mar
El mar abierto de par en par
He ahí el mar quebrado de repente
Para que el ojo vea el comienzo del mundo
He ahí el mar
De una ola a la otra hay el tiempo de la vida
De sus olas a mis ojos hay la distancia de la muerte

ERAMOS LOS ELEGIDOS DEL SOL

Eramos los elegidos del sol
Y no nos dimos cuenta
Fuimos los elegidos de la más alta estrella
Y no supimos responder a su regalo
Angustia de impotencia
El agua nos amaba
La tierra nos amaba
Las selvas eran nuestras
El éxtasis era nuestro espacio propio
Tu mirada era el universo frente a frente
Tu belleza era el sonido del amanecer
La primavera amada por los árboles
Ahora somos una tristeza contagiosa
Una muerte antes de tiempo
El alma que no sabe en qué sitio se encuentra
El invierno en los huesos sin un relámpago
Y todo esto porque tú no supiste lo que es la eternidad
Ni comprendiste el alma de mi alma en su barco de tinieblas
En su trono de águila herida de infinito

Or the beginning of death deeper than yourself
And higher than all the mountains
What is there on the other side
The millennial desire to make a form and a rhythm
Or the eternal whirlwind of broken petals

Here's the sea
The sea wide open
The sea suddenly burst open
So the eye can see the beginning of the world
Here's the sea
From one wave to the next is the space of a lifetime
From your waves to my eyes is the distance of death   [D.M.G.]

WE WERE THE SUN'S CHOSEN ONES

We were the sun's chosen ones
And we didn't know it
We were the highest star's elected
And we didn't know how to answer its gift
Anguish of impotence
Water loved us
The earth loved us
The woods were ours
Ecstasy was our only home
Your glance was the universe face to face
Your beauty was the sound of the dawn
Spring was loved by the trees
Now we are just a contagious grief
A death before its time
The soul that doesn't know where it is
Winter in the bones without a flash of lightning
And all this because you didn't know what eternity was
You didn't understand the soul of my soul on its ship of darkness
On its eagle's throne wounded by the infinite   [D.M.G.]

EL PASO DEL RETORNO

A RAQUEL QUE ME DIJO UN DÍA "CUANDO TÚ TE
ALEJAS UN SOLO INSTANTE, EL TIEMPO Y YO LLORAMOS"

Yo soy ese que salió hace un año de su tierra
Buscando lejanías de vida y muerte
Su propio corazón y el corazón del mundo
Cuando el viento silbaba entrañas
En un crepúsculo gigante y sin recuerdos

Guiado por mi estrella
Con el pecho vacío
Y los ojos clavados en la altura
Salí hacia mi destino

Oh mis buenos amigos
¿Me habéis reconocido?
He vivido una vida que no puede vivirse
Pero tú Poesía no me has abandonado un solo instante

Oh mis amigos aquí estoy
Vosotros sabéis acaso lo que yo era
Pero nadie sabe lo que soy
El viento me hizo viento
La sombra me hizo sombra
El horizonte me hizo horizonte preparado a todo
La tarde me hizo tarde
Y el alba me hizo alba para cantar de nuevo

Oh poeta esos tremendos ojos
Ese andar de alma de acero y de bondad de mármol
Este es aquel que llegó al final del último camino
Y que vuelve quizás con otro paso
Hago al andar el ruido de la muerte
Y si mis ojos os dicen
Cuánta vida he vivido y cuánta muerte he muerto
Ellos podrían también deciros
Cuánta vida he muerto y cuánta muerte he vivido

¡Oh mis fantasmas! ¡Oh mis queridos espectros!
La noche ha dejado noche en mis cabellos

THE RETURN PASSAGE

FOR RAQUEL, WHO TOLD ME ONE DAY "WHEN YOU GO
AWAY FOR JUST AN INSTANT, BOTH TIME AND I WEEP"

I am the one who left his land one year ago
Searching for distances of life and death
For his own heart and the heart of the world
When the wind whistled entrails
In a dawn gigantic and without memories

Guided by my star
With empty breast
And eyes fixed on the sky
I set out toward my destiny

Oh my good friends
Have you recognized me?
I have lived a life that can't be lived
But you Poetry you have not abandoned me for a single moment

Oh my friends here I am
You know what I was perhaps
But no one knows what I am
The wind made me wind
The shadow made me shadow
The horizon made me horizon ready for everything
The night made me night
And the dawn made me dawn so I could sing again

Oh poet those tremendous eyes
That walk of steel soul and marble grace
This is the one who came to the end of the last road
And returns perhaps with just another step
I make the sound of death as I walk
And if my eyes tell you
How much life I have lived and how much death I have died
They can also tell you
How much life I have died and how much death I have lived

Oh my phantoms! Oh my cherished dreams!
The night has left night in my hair

¿En dónde estuve? ¿Por dónde he andado?
¿Pero era ausencia aquélla o era mayor presencia?

Cuando las piedras oyen mi paso
Sienten una ternura que les ensancha el alma
Se hacen señas furtivas y hablan bajo:
Allí se acerca el buen amigo
El hombre de las distancias
Que viene fatigado de tanta muerte al hombro
De tanta vida en el pecho
Y busca donde pasar la noche

Heme aquí ante vuestros limpios ojos
Heme aquí vestido de lejanías
Atrás quedaron los negros nubarrones
Los años de tinieblas en el antro olvidado
Traigo un alma lavada por el fuego
Vosotros me llamáis sin saber a quién llamáis
Traigo un cristal sin sombra un corazón que no decae
La imagen de la nada y un rostro que sonríe
Traigo un amor muy parecido al universo
La Poesía me despejó el camino
Ya no hay banalidades en mi vida
¿Quién guió mis pasos de modo tan certero?

Mis ojos dicen a aquellos que cayeron
Disparad contra mí vuestros dardos
Vengad en mí vuestras angustias
Vengad en mí vuestros fracasos
Yo soy invulnerable
He tomado mi sitio en el cielo como el silencio

Los siglos de la tierra me caen en los brazos
Yo soy amigos el viajero sin fin
Las alas de la enorme aventura
Batían entre inviernos y veranos
Mirad cómo suben estrellas en mi alma
Desde que he expulsado las serpientes del tiempo obscurecido

¿Cómo podremos entendernos?
Heme aquí de regreso de donde no se vuelve
Compasión de las olas y piedad de los astros

Where was I? Where have I been?
And was it absence or greater presence?

When the stones hear my step
They feel a softness which fills their soul
They make secret signs and speak below:
Here comes our good friend
The man from the distances
Who comes tired from so much death on his shoulders
From so much life in his heart
And he's looking for a place to spend the night

Here I am before your clear eyes
Here I am dressed in distant places
The black thunderclouds left behind
Years of darkness in the forgotten cave
I bring a soul washed with fire
You call me without knowing who you call
I bring a crystal without darkness a heart that doesn't decay
The image of nothingness and a face that smiles
I bring a love much like the universe
Poetry cleared the way for me
There are no banalities in my life now
Who guided my steps in such a certain way?

My eyes call to those that have fallen
Shoot your arrows at me
Avenge your sorrows in me
Avenge your failures in me
I am invulnerable
Like silence I have taken my place in the sky

The earth's centuries fall in my arms
I am my friends the endless traveller
The wings of the great adventure
Beat through winters and summers
Watch how stars climb in my soul
Since I have expelled the serpents of darkened time

How will we understand ourselves?
Here I am back from where no one returns
Compassion of waves pity of stars

¡Cuánto tiempo perdido! Este es el hombre de las lejanías
El que daba vuelta las páginas de los muertos
Sin tiempo sin espacio sin corazón sin sangre
El que andaba de un lado para otro
Desesperado y solo en las tinieblas
Solo en el vacío
Como un perro que ladra hacia el fondo de un abismo

¡Oh vosotros! ¡Oh mis buenos amigos!
Los que habéis tocado mis manos
¿Qué habéis tocado?
Y vosotros que habéis escuchado mi voz
¿Qué habéis escuchado?
Y los que habéis contemplado mis ojos
¿Qué habéis contemplado?

Lo he perdido todo y todo lo he ganado
Y ni siquiera pido
La parte de la vida que me corresponde
Ni montañas de fuego ni mares cultivados
Es tanto más lo que he ganado que lo que he perdido
Así es el viaje al fin del mundo
Y ésta es la corona de sangre de la gran experiencia
La corona regalo de mi estrella
¿En dónde estuve en dónde estoy?

Los árboles lloran un pájaro canta inconsolable
Decid ¿quién es el muerto?
El viento me solloza
¡Qué inquietudes me has dado!
Algunas flores exclaman
¿Estás vivo aún?
¿Quién es el muerto entonces?
Las aguas gimen tristemente
¿Quién ha muerto en estas tierras?

Ahora sé lo que soy y lo que era
Conozco la distancia que va del hombre a la verdad
Conozco la palabra que aman los muertos
Este es el que ha llorado el mundo el que ha llorado resplandores

How much time lost! This is the man from the distances
The one who crossed the pages of the dead
Without time without space without heart without blood
The one who walked from one side to the other
Hopeless and alone in the darkness
Alone in the emptiness
Like a dog howling at the bottom of a void

Oh you! Oh my good friends!
You who have touched my hands
What have you touched?
And you who have heard my voice
What have you heard?
And those who have looked into my eyes
What have you looked into?

I have lost it all and I have gained it all
And I ask for nothing not even
The share of life which is mine
Nor the mountains of fire nor the cultivated seas
I've gained so much more than I've lost
That's how the journey to the end of the world is
And this is the great experience's crown of blood
The crown gift of my star
Where was I where am I?

The trees weep a bird sings inconsolable
Tell me who's the dead one?
The wind sobs
What madness have you brought me!
Some flowers call
You're still alive?
Who's the dead one then?
The waters sadly howl
Who has died in these parts?

Now I know what I am and what I was
I know the distance that runs from a man to the truth
I know the word the dead love best
This is the one who wept the world the one who wept bright stars

Las lágrimas se hinchan se dilatan
Y empiezan a girar sobre su eje
Heme aquí ante vosotros
Cómo podremos entendernos Cómo saber lo que decimos
Hay tantos muertos que me llaman
Allí donde la tierra pierde su ruido
Allí donde me esperan mis queridos fantasmas
Mis queridos espectros
Miradme os amo tanto pero soy extranjero
¿Quién salió de su tierra
Sin saber el hondor de su aventura?
Al desplegar las alas
El mismo no sabía qué vuelo era su vuelo

Vuestro tiempo y vuestro espacio
No son mi espacio ni mi tiempo
¿Quién es el extranjero? ¿Reconocéis su andar?
Es el que vuelve con un sabor de eternidad en la garganta
Con un olor de olvido en los cabellos
Con un sonar de venas misteriosas
Es este que está llorando el universo
Que sobrepasó la muerte y el rumor de la selva secreta
Soy impalpable ahora como ciertas semillas
Que el viento mismo que las lleva no las siente
Oh Poesía nuestro reino empieza

Este es aquel que durmió muchas veces
Allí donde hay que estar alerta
Donde las rocas prohíben la palabra
Allí donde se confunde la muerte con el canto del mar
Ahora vengo a saber que fui a buscar las llaves
He aquí las llaves
¿Quién las había perdido?
¿Cuánto tiempo ha que se perdieron?
Nadie encontró las llaves perdidas en el tiempo y en las brumas
¡Cuántos siglos perdidas!
Al fondo de las tumbas
Al fondo de los mares
Al fondo del murmullo de los vientos
Al fondo del silencio
He aquí los signos

The tears swell they expand
And they begin to spin on their axis
Here I am before you
How will we understand ourselves How to know what we say
So many dead are calling out to me
There where the earth loses its noise
There where my cherished phantoms await me
My cherished dreams
Look at me I love you so much but am a stranger
Who left his land
Not knowing the depth of his adventure?
Even when he spread his wings
He didn't know which flight was his flight

Your time and your space
Are not my space or my time
Who is the stranger? Do you recognize his step?
He is the one returning with a taste of eternity in his throat
With a scent of oblivion in his hair
With a rushing of mysterious veins
He is the one who is weeping the world
The one who went beyond death and the rumor of the secret forest
I am impalpable now like certain seeds
Which even the wind as it carries them never touches
Oh Poetry our reign begins

This is the one who slept so many times
Where one must stay alert
Where the rocks forbid the word
There where death is confused with the singing of the sea
Now I understand that I went to search for the keys
Here are the keys
Who lost them?
How long were they lost?
No one found the keys lost in time and fog
How many centuries lost!
At the bottom of tombs
At the bottom of seas
At the bottom of the winds' cry
At the bottom of silence
Here are the signs

¡Cuánto tiempo olvidados!
Pero entonces amigo ¿qué vas a decirnos?
¿Quién ha de comprenderte? ¿De dónde vienes?
¿En dónde estabas? ¿En qué alturas en qué profundidades?
Andaba por la Historia del brazo con la muerte

Oh hermano nada voy a decirte
Cuando hayas tocado lo que nadie puede tocar
Más que el árbol te gustará callar

Forgotten so long!
But then friend, what are you going to tell us?
Who has to understand you? Where do you come from?
Where were you? In what heights in what depths?
I passed through History arm in arm with death

O brother I'll tell you nothing
When you have seen what no one else can see
You'll want to be more silent than the tree   [D.M.G.]

Farewell

HASTA LUEGO

La mariposa boreal se acerca y el candor
Y gira sobre su eje geológico con un halo
Antes que la flor helicóptera que seguimos con los ojos
En la dirección del apacible perfume sin capa
Se caiga de su cráter

La sangre de la montaña brota inagotable
A causa de sus flores y sus olvidos
Bajo la calma mirada del viento

Qué altura me dais para el veraneo del cráneo
Os desafío a todos os desafío
El pájaro pondrá su huevo sobre el porvenir
Gritando Tanto peor

Os traigo los recuerdos de Altazor
Que jugaba con las golondrinas y los cementerios
Los molinos las tardes y las tumbas como bolsillos del mar
Os traigo un saludo de Altazor
Que se fue de su carne al viento estupefacto
Hasta luego señores
Hasta luego árboles y piedras

de Ver y Palpar, *1941*

FAREWELL

The northern butterfly draws near and there's innocence at last
Spinning on its geological axis with a halo
Before the helicopter flower we're following with our eyes
In the direction of the gentle and unmasked scent
Falls from its crater

The mountain's blood flows without end
Beneath the calm glance of the wind
Because of its flowers and its neglect

What heights you give me for the skull's holidays
I challenge you I challenge you all
The bird will lay its egg on the future
Screaming So much the worse

I bring you regards from Altazor
The one who played with the swallows and the cemeteries
The mills the afternoons and the graves like pockets of the sea
I bring you greetings from Altazor
The one who left his skin for the stupefied sky
Good-bye gentlemen
Good-bye trees
          Good-bye stones   [D.M.G.]

from To See and Feel, *1941*

The Works of
Vicente Huidobro

Ecos del Alma, Santiago, Chile, 1911.

Canciones en la Noche, Santiago, Chile, 1913.

La Gruta de Silencio, Santiago, Chile, 1913.

Pasando y Pasando, (chronicles and commentaries), Santiago, Chile, 1914.

Las Pagodas Ocultas, (psalms, prose poems, essays, and parables), Santiago, Chile, 1914.

Adán, Santiago, Chile, 1916.

El Espejo de Agua, Editorial Orión, Buenos Aires, 1916.

Horizon Carré, Editions Paul Birault, Paris, 1917.

Tour Eiffel, Imprenta Pueyo, Madrid, 1918.

Hallali, Ediciones Jesús López, Madrid, 1918.

Ecuatorial, Imprenta Pueyo, Madrid, 1918.

Poemas Articos, Imprenta Pueyo, Madrid, 1918.

Saisons Choisies, (an anthology of earlier poems selected and translated into the French by the author himself), Editions Le Cible, Paris, 1921.

Salle 14, (an exhibition of "painted poems"), Théâtre Edouard VII, Paris, 1922.

Finis Britanniae: A Redoubtable Secret Society Directed Against English Imperialism, (novelistic essays), Editions Fiat Lux, Paris, 1923.

Automne Régulier, Editions Librairie de France, Paris, 1925.

Tout A Coup, Editions Au Sans Pareil, Paris, 1925.

Manifestes, (manifestos and essays on poetry), Editions de la Revue Mondiale, Paris, 1925.

Vientos Contrarios, (essays and aphorisms), Editorial Nascimento, Santiago, Chile, 1926.

Mío Cid Campeador, (novel), Compañía Iberoamericana de Publicaciones, S.A., Madrid, 1929.

Altazor, Compañía Iberoamericana de Publicaciones, S.A., Madrid, 1931.

Temblor de Cielo, Editorial Plutarco, S.A., Madrid, 1931.

The Mirror of a Mage, (Cagliostro), translated by Warre B. Wells, Eyre and Spottiswoode, London, 1931; Houghton Mifflin, New York, 1931.

Portrait of a Paladin, (Mío Cid Campeador), translated by Warre B. Wells, Eyre and Spottiswoode, London, 1931; Horace Liverwright, New York, 1932.

Tremblement de Ciel, (French version of *Temblor De Cielo* translated by the author), Editions de L'As de Coeur, Paris, 1932.

Gilles De Raíz, (play), Editions Totem, Paris, 1932.

Cagliostro, (film-novel), Editorial Zig-Zag, S.A., Santiago, Chile, 1934.

La Próxima: Historia Que Pasó en Poco Tiempo Más, (novel), Ediciones Walton, Santiago, Chile, 1934.

Papá o el Diario de Alicia Mir, (novel), Ediciones Walton, Santiago, Chile, 1934.

En La Luna, (play), Editorial Ercilla, Santiago, Chile, 1934.

Tres Inmensas Novelas: Tres Novelas Ejemplares, (short novels written in collaboration with Hans Arp), Editorial Zig-Zag, S.A., Santiago, Chile, 1935.

Sátiro o el Poder de las Palabras, (novel), Editorial Zig-Zag, S.A., Santiago, Chile, 1939.

Ver y Palpar, Ediciones Ercilla, Santiago, Chile, 1941.

El Ciudadano del Olvido, Ediciones Ercilla, Santiago, Chile, 1941.

Antología de Vicente Huidobro, (prologue, selection, translation, and notes by Eduardo Anguita), Editorial Zig-Zag, S.A., Santiago, Chile, 1945.

Ultimos Poemas, (posthumously published), Talleres Gráficos Ahués Hnos., Santiago, Chile, 1948.

Obras Completas de Vicente Huidobro, (prologue by Braulio Arenas), Editorial Zig-Zag, S.A., Santiago, Chile, 1964.

Obras Completas de Vicente Huidobro, (prologue by Hugo Montes), Editorial Andres Bello, Santiago, Chile, 1976.

BIBLIOGRAPHY

The most complete bibliography of Huidobro's life and work was compiled by Nicholas Hey, "Bibliografía de y sobre Vicente Huidobro," and published in *Revista Iberoamericana,* Vol. XLI, Num. 91, April–June, 1975, University of Pittsburgh, Pittsburgh, Pennsylvania.